To Gill

The ChapWell Method

Method

The 7 Keys to Happiness, Wellbeing and Success

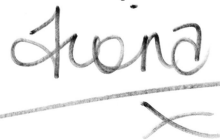

with every best wish and thanks for soooo.... much

Fiona Chapman

Fiona

x

First published by Completely Novel

ISBN: 978-1-8491480-6-1

Book cover designed by
Sheila Marshall Designs

Book design by Shore Books and Design,
Blackborough End, Norfolk PE32 1SF

Contents

Foreword

Whoever coined that term 'the jungle of life', for me, was spot on and certainly knew the possibilities that life could bring, both good and bad. This book is all about how to 'do' your jungle journey to suit your unique needs and enable you to enjoy all life has to offer. The ChapWell Method 7 keys enable you to be your own life coach, showing you how to tap into your unique power and break away from those draining states such as stress, loss of confidence or worse still fear!

My method doesn't pretend that life is always rosy rather it shows you how to live a successful and happy life in your own way. My main aim in this book is to give you a set of tools or strategies that allow you to steer your way through the challenging times, the disappointments and go for your hopes and dreams so that you can thrive not just survive. Whatever success, happiness and well-being means for you this method helps you to create it. The simple exercises have been adapted and designed by me through my many years of working with myself, leading and managing teams and working with a wide range of clients both one to one and in groups.

I love to hear from people who are following the ChapWell Method, how they are getting along, and encourage you to keep in touch. Let me know how things are going for you via my website www.chapwellmethod.com. Sign up for my free, monthly newsletter where I feature exercises in response to followers' requests, enabling you to add to the wealth of techniques and tools you already have for free. Send in your requests for specific exercises to support your progress. I pick one a month and design an exercise to help keep you growing on the road to your success, happiness and wellbeing.

Acknowledgements

First my grateful thanks goes to the team who helped me get this book into a decent shape bringing it to life from my boxes of exercises, training and coaching notes. It follows then I have to acknowledge gratefully all of those people who have worked with me or have been a part of my life in many other guises helping me develop my skills and share those skills with more and more people.

I really appreciate all the support and help from my family especially Stephen, Peter, Natalie, Mick and Caty who never once questioned if I could do it just when will it be finished! I'm forever grateful to all my friends who continue to support me, make me laugh and stop me getting too serious or working too hard! Special thanks to Jane, Margaret and the 3 Sues. Especially Sue H for keeping it real and looking forward to finding my book in the local charity shop and the Marr for pointing out that lions don't live in the jungle!

Finally, I'd like to dedicate this book to my Mr Philip, miss you loads, and I know you'd be so proud of me.

Chapter 1

The Jungle of Life

I'm Fiona Chapman and I designed the ChapWell Method as a direct result of working with myself, and others, helping them to be the best they can be and create the life that works for them. I'm not here to tell you how to live your life, just to give you a toolbox so you can craft and design your life to experience your happiness, success and wellbeing. Not mine but yours! That's what I love about the ChapWell Method; it allows you to design and create your life, not mine or some other guru's life.

I have really struggled to get a nice sharp introduction to this book. *'Just explain in a few sentences what you are offering'* has been the advice of my helpful business coach. Yet it seems I want to tell you in paragraphs not sentences. Then my coach asked me repeatedly to identify my niche market. As you can see from my clients' testimonials there are no niches: just everyday people, all ages from 27 to 83, male and female and a range of ethnic origins. A pretty normal bunch of people looking to get much more out of life and to be able to roll with the punches no matter what life brings them: challenging times and good times. So I decided to let one of my clients tell you what the ChapWell Method is all about and this is what she said:

> *'Fiona has a programme to enable people to relax and deal with whatever is upsetting them at the moment. This programme can work in any situation*

because it is designed just for you and your needs. As well as the hypnotherapy you will receive bespoke visualisation exercises for you to work on. The therapy itself is no different from sitting in a chair and having some sound advice given to you. The difference is that really the advice comes from within your own self, compiled from all the words and feelings that you already know and feel. Just try it and see how you feel after a few days.' – Jean

And then I asked two of my course delegates:

'It's just so lovely to be able to feel calm and relaxed at the flick of a switch, just a thought. I feel so much more confident now that whatever comes up I'll be able to deal with it and better than that I know I have the answers if you know what I mean, it's like I know and feel how to be OK now. Before I used to worry about things, I knew I shouldn't but now I know how to smile inside and out.' – Emma

'It's like the job I went for and got, it was like I was able to do and say all the right things, before I would have panicked, messed up the interview and spent the rest of the day sure I didn't stand a chance. Instead I had to wait 2 weeks to hear I'd got the job but you know I felt really calm about it, sure I'd done my best and if it wasn't to be then it wasn't because of my interview.' – Adrian

I choose to work with people who are willing to take action, not willing to accept the status quo. People who figure there must be a better way to 'do' life and get what they want and need from their life if only they could figure out 'the magic' of how to do it, or download a happiness and wellbeing CD into their mind. This is about how you can make the journey of life just as much fun and reward as the bright shiny moments are, experiencing the challenging times as no more than a part of life, even as times that help us grow in confidence and learn rather than be the robbers of our happiness, wellbeing and purpose.

Here's a bit more about me just so you know who you are working with on your journey through the jungle of life. I have worked for more than 30 years in education and training as a leader, manager, trainer and teacher. Since the 80s I have been training people to develop their skills to excel at work and in their personal life. As time moved on I started to attract clients on a one-to-one basis, coaching them through their unique issues and showing them how to develop their ability to coach themselves. After all, it's up to us to keep our bodies healthy and fit, so why don't we have the same approach to our mental strength and wellbeing? Most of us understand the basic elements at least of the necessity for a healthy, well balanced diet and the importance of regular exercise. So it follows we should be able to apply the same ongoing care to securing our wellbeing mentally. Besides, it's a thought that drives us to eat healthily, and another thought that gets us exercising, so how can we make sure our minds support us and play their role in our wellbeing, happiness and goals? After all, even the simplest of lives has its ups and downs and as the song says, 'When the going gets tough the tough get going'. So how do we keep ourselves tough?

My approach comes from many areas: neurolinguistic programming, emotional intelligence, motivational dialogue, language and mind techniques, autogenics, hypnotherapy, reiki, cognitive behavioural therapy, mindfulness, psychology, and the list goes on. I created the ChapWell Method as a combination of many -ologies and life experience, and it made sense to give my approach and methods a name of its own.

During the 80s and 90s part of my work was leading and managing teams of managers, trainers and teachers who taught in a wide range of subjects from Latin to yoga. The thing that struck me most was that when any change in working practice was needed it was always the yoga teachers who were the most stressed out. Up until then I'd always thought yoga teachers must be the most relaxed people on the planet but no, it seems they were relaxed only when they were doing yoga. Added to that, their experience of stress had probably led them to practise yoga. I began to wonder if there is a way to experience peace and calm, a most desirable state and the optimum state for performance and learning as part of everyday life. Now before I find myself overwhelmed by irate yoga followers and teachers, please understand, I am an advocate of yoga and all other relaxing practices. What I wanted was to be able to create that feeling of peace and calm as my default setting, available to me all of the time, so that by just a single thought we could experience calm and peace in our mind and body. This would free us from the physical and mental blockages caused by stress, tension, worry, irritation, whatever you want to call that state that takes away the enjoyment from your day. This ability to create peace and calm as and when you want it naturally became the cornerstone for the ChapWell Method.

Why peace and calm?

I believe that stress is our biggest enemy in the modern world. So many of our problems and challenges rely on our confidence, focus and peace of mind to solve them; how can we do that to the best of our ability and stay strong if stress is chipping away at us? Too much stress just takes us apart: unable to really think straight and focus, worry distracts and robs us of enjoying whatever we are doing, even at times when we are supposedly relaxing and recharging. How many times have you managed to achieve peace and calm, had a lovely time and then had to move your mind back to the issues of the day and felt the tension and stress coming along too? Maybe it's work, family concerns, things you must/want to get done and all those things we think we ought to do? How would you feel if you could really carry on with your day with a peaceful, calm mindset? How do you think you would feel if you could summon that feeling just by the flick of a thought? I just wonder how focused, productive and happy you would feel if you were confident, calm and at peace with yourself? You probably know if you practice yoga, but what if you could create that feeling most of the time?

Stress myths

Sometimes people say to me, 'Oh, I need stress to get me motivated'. I understand that, but are you using stress as a stick to beat yourself up with, to perform, meet that deadline, find a solution, cope, overcome your fears and worries? Or do you support yourself with a carrot in the shape of peace and calm and then pour in positive, motivating energy to get you where you want and feeling great whilst you journey through the jungle? This allows you to focus, create a relaxed state and choose an 'even keel' as your default setting so you can truly focus on the now, on what you are doing, and who you are with. Happiness experts state that 40% of our happiness quota is genetic, 10% is environmental, with a whopping 50% available to us to tip the balance in the direction we want. So what balance do you want to choose? Wellbeing and happiness or all the other downer states that at some time or other you've probably experienced? Do nothing and you'll not only get the same but probably more too!

The 'tip the balance' techniques

In a nutshell, as I have said before, all of the techniques and methods developed through this system are ones that I have used on myself, my clients and my courses. Like all of us I have a story but this book is about you and what is next for you, so I'm not going to bore you with more than a brief explanation. Suffice to say that up until my late thirties I had navigated some good times and the usual not-so-good times in the shape of a challenging childhood, loneliness, isolation, physical and mental illness, divorce, financial difficulties, single parenthood, unsatisfactory relationships etc. One very kind friend once commented that I could rival the soaps! That made me sit up straight!

After making another major relationship mistake, I decided to go it alone and work on myself. I recognised the only constant in all of these times was me and that, in truth, is the only thing any of us have control over in life. So it was time to work on me and from those roots, my studies, training and development, the ChapWell Method began to take shape. Just a postscript to that sorry tale of woe: my career continued to flourish during the hard times and good times, so I knew I had it in me to manage 'Project Fiona'! I also knew I could cope, but why was I always coping with bad stuff?

My methods certainly worked for me, and then without really trying I started to attract one-to-one clients and it seemed obvious to me that the techniques could easily be learnt on a course. So the courses began and it made sense to bundle them up into one method, as the ChapWell Method is not about one therapy, but a combination designed for you to tailor to meet your unique needs, your life and your journey through the jungle of life. It never ceases to amaze me how quickly people pick up the techniques and start using them to suit themselves. I absolutely love it when young people join the course too, as I didn't really start to get going with my life or really enjoying my life until my early forties. What a waste, but there you go!

Are you willing to take action? Dare you question your status quo?

This approach enables you to make rapid changes and enjoy peace and deep relaxation whilst bringing more of what you want into your life. Not only do you discover the ways within yourself to move forward and solve your challenges, but you also learn and gather about you a clever set of skills and strategies to help you avoid getting bogged down next time life throws a curveball your way. Because let's face it – life's like that!

Doesn't it make sense to equip yourself to thrive and succeed when you are looking for more from life? It's much better than waiting for a challenging time when all our energy goes into coping with the problem and the stress that brings us down, just when we need to be in top form to navigate ourselves through a tricky patch. I wonder how you'd feel if there were no tricky patches, just opportunities to grow and learn? Maybe you've heard that before, but what if it could be true for you? What if you had everything you need to 'do' life brilliantly but you just didn't know how to access and use everything you have? Well, that's what the ChapWell Method gives you: a way to do life, deal with your challenges, big or small, to thrive and succeed. I just wonder how you would feel if you knew that whatever life held you could handle it, cope, and more than that, thrive!

The lion and the ChapWell Method

You may wonder why the lion is on the cover of my book. Well, just think about the lion in the jungle: he strides through, sure of his right to be there, sure of who he is, a lion. A lion that is the king of the jungle, no better than others, but king of his role and purpose in life, sure of himself, confidently striding through the jungle. Calm and self-assured and just getting on with what lions do: hunt, eat, laze in the sun, rest and enjoy the company of their pride.

The only time I have ever seen a stressed lion is when they are in a cage and not allowed or able to flow with their true nature. They are held in an unnatural environment, behind bars, never able to live the life they were born to live, and maybe they just give up and loll around, sleeping their life away until it's all over. Once I stood in front of a lion's cage, and the lion just looked at me as if he didn't see me. For a moment I just wondered who was in the cage, was it me or the lion? My bars were of my own making, crafted from my fears, my beliefs that who I was wasn't enough, and all I had to do was escape from the cage. The lion's cage was real and solid; my bars were just as solid though crafted in my mind. I just needed to work out the magic to melt them away, to be able to stride, like a lion, confident and sure through the jungle of life. The lion's fears were the cage, which was real, and mine were the jungle and, though just thoughts, were just as real. So if my mind could create the bars, I figured, if directed in the right way, my mind could melt the bars and allow me to enjoy the jungle.

If you've ever been to a jungle you'll know it is a wonderful place, beautiful, peaceful and teeming with colour and life. However, like the lion, you need to be confident you have the right equipment, skills and tools to travel the jungle safely. Have you got the tools and confidence to travel the jungle of life, sure that no matter what, you'll cope and more than that, you'll thrive? I just wonder what you'd choose: a view of the jungle through your bars or a wonderful journey through the jungle, enjoying all it has to offer?

Big or small stuff

It was really important to me that this method should be a lifetime set of tools and techniques. I have studied in many different 'mind' areas and spent many happy hours in the classroom developing, learning and fine tuning my skills. What has amazed me is how few people have packaged courses focused on, and grounded in, 'How to do everyday life and the challenges of life'. Furthermore, many of my fellow students in their practice seem to fail to apply the tools learnt to everyday life, preferring just the crisis moments. To explain myself let me give you some examples of how I have used the tools just lately.

Yesterday I had one of my least favourite things, the dentist. Don't get me wrong, my dentist is very good and never causes me any pain, but I can think of better things to do than sit for 40 minutes in a dentist chair whilst I undergo the joy of a root filling. So I used Key 1, the easy step to relaxation, and enjoyed 40 minutes of peace and calm, only coming back to reality when my dentist repeatedly asked me to rinse as he was finished. I think he thought I'd fallen asleep!

Currently I am living in a building site so I can have a home that suits me and my work. This is a big project, a whole house renovation, and it is the first time I have done anything like this, and added to that it's winter, cold and damp. Three months in and the dream is grounded in reality, over budget, over time, etc, etc. There are highs and lows and brilliant builders but all the time I've known this is doable and, more than that, I'm happy, I'm creating my dream and solving the problems as I go. Peace and calm surrounds me and when it doesn't I can and do bring it into my reality using the 7 keys as and when needed. I'd never have taken on something like this without the ChapWell Method.

On top of all this, I am working and writing a book in my spare time, and I am making my life and dreams work by steering my thoughts about my current living conditions towards creating my life the way I want it. No, it's not perfect (whose life is), but yes, I just know it will all be OK and I'll sort the challenges as they come and enjoy doing it! So that's what I mean when I say the perfect set of tools and techniques for you, no matter what you are doing, where you are going and where you have been. There is a common belief that you have the potential for everything you need in life within you – such as confidence, happiness, focus, peacefulness, the ability to learn and so on, but what if you just have not learnt how to access or use them? Basically that's what the ChapWell Method is all about; it just shows you how to access your own potential, let it work for you and build your life how you want it to be. It lets you in on the secret of how to manage your 'magic'! OK, it's not really magic, it's just learning how to use your mind to support you rather than stop you! Deep in our minds, or in our subconscious, we have programmes and patterns of thinking that we have learnt as we grew and matured and gathered life experience.

Success or Failure or Feedback

Sometimes these programmes our minds run don't suit our lives now and can be programmes learnt from other people's fears, our own fears and from what I call '2 and 2 make 5' life experiences. For example, maybe you had a bad experience on public transport. You moved to a new area, caught the wrong bus, got lost, and wondered if you would ever reach home (I'm talking about me here) and five hours later after a long, frightening walk home in the dark, somehow you got there. Your mind has a choice on how to catalogue this experience: do you opt for 'Public transport is dangerous, frightening and you can't do it, something will go wrong if you catch a bus, you can't trust yourself to get it right' or do you choose to programme your mind with reinforcing thoughts of 'How resourceful you are, how you sorted the problem even though it took a long time, how brave you were walking the streets at night, how you can deal with things that go wrong and be successful'? I just wonder what learning would feed your mind? Would this event set you up for success or pull you down?

Keep the good stuff

Let's be clear here, a lot of these programmes or strategies we learnt are very useful, essential to our success, survival and wellbeing. We learnt that fire burns and we automatically conduct ourselves accordingly and this keeps us safe. Sometimes, though, we have programmes running that may not be true for our lives and hopes now. Then what happens? Despite our very best efforts, we can find ourselves unable to change, to adapt, to grow to suit our current life experience and therefore unable to build the life we want. Maybe you learnt from an early age to worry, to expect the worst. My question is, does it work for you, does this support your happiness, wellbeing and a successful life for you now? If your answer is 'Yes' that's fine, but if your answer is 'No, but I can't stop', then my method shows you 'how to stop' or rather, reprogramme your thinking to suit you. This is where the 'magic' of self-hypnosis works, allowing you to gently reprogramme your thinking to meet the needs of your life now, to suit you and the uniqueness of you. Who else knows what's best for you and what you want and need but you? Who else is best placed to find out what you need, want and have the potential for?

Be the lion in your life

How do you live like the lion then? Maybe it is a hobby or maybe it is a favourite piece of music or a television programme where you can lose yourself totally in what you are doing. No angst, no threats, no deadlines, just totally absorbed in what you are doing. Do you feel stressed or are you just being and doing what you do? I wonder, if you brought that frame of mind to every part of your life how you would feel, think and be? Or maybe if you could move yourself into a relaxed, focused mindset when needed – how would your life be?

Wondering about self-hypnosis?

With the ChapWell Method you first learn the secrets of deep relaxation and self-hypnosis to create a peaceful and calm state of mind; this is the first key of the 7-key system. Some people query this starting point, either saying they don't believe in self-hypnosis or hypnosis itself.

Hypnosis is just a trance-like state, or altered state, exactly like the state you enter just before you fall asleep; you are still aware and able to respond but your conscious mind is totally relaxed. If you have been deep in thought, miles away, when someone has interrupted your thoughts, this is an example of a trance-like state. When you daydream, you are moving your mind into another place, your daydream, and this happens by using self-hypnosis, bypassing or relaxing the conscious mind. By relaxing the conscious mind you are working directly with the subconscious where your longer, stronger memories, programmes and patterns of thinking are held. The subconscious accepts your thoughts more easily as it relies on the critical mind to do the sifting and sorting of what is OK to go into the subconscious, our long-term memory and life programming store place.

All these are ways of being that you have already probably experienced, certainly just before going to sleep. Remember you are absolutely in control all of the time; this is not stage hypnosis! Stage hypnotists select willing volunteers, who by volunteering have given permission for their thoughts to be directed by another. They also select those most willing to please, follow instructions and therefore work with people who don't mind following their instructions, however absurd. The only person giving the instructions with the ChapWell Method is you, so you are perfectly safe. If you imagine something you don't like, just change it to something you do want and like!

Incidentally, many of my clients and those attending my courses report improvements in the quality of their sleep after using the techniques.

Have a go at using self-hypnosis (trance work) and create a little extra happiness in your day right now.

Exercise

Creating Happiness

This exercise gets you started using those fabulous assets – your imagination and life experience. It only takes a few minutes and remember it's self-hypnosis too!

1. Make sure you are safe to close your eyes and go inward in your mind. If you find closing your eyes difficult just stare at a fixed point; that works fine too.

2. Now pull up a memory of when you felt happy; it could have been an event, or listening to music, any time that your mind gives you.

3. Imagine you are in that memory; feel the feelings linked with your happy memory.

4. When you feel yourself smiling, enjoying that happy feeling, notice how happiness feels for you.

5. Now come back into the now, bringing that feeling of happiness with you.

I have used this exercise many times and some find it easier than others but all end up smiling! That's fine; this is all about you and developing your wonderful ability to find your own happiness and create your own life easily and effortlessly.

You are now officially in training. Over the next few days, do this exercise whenever you have a few spare minutes. By training your mind to recognise and get used to your happiness feelings you are forming a happiness feeling habit. This is so easy that you can do it without spending much time or changing your days; your mind 'gym' is instantly available to you with no need to travel, book in or find another hour or two in your day.

Relaxation and self-hypnosis

The two major tools you will learn and use are relaxation and self-hypnosis. The ultimate state for learning and implementing change, relaxation restores and revives, so you feel the benefits from the first exercise you try. You will change, but that's what you want, isn't it? You now have a choice: keep on doing the same things or do something different and start feeling an amazing shift in your life. With the 7 keys as your guide, you will use your powerful mind and your wonderful imagination to create your unique happiness and wellbeing; not mine but yours.

Learn to leave the struggle in the past. Every time I work with a new client or a new course group I am amazed how quickly people pick up the techniques and start creating for themselves the life they want, allowing them to change, grow and develop as they learn to direct their mind and become the director of their life.

Sophie Keller, author of the 'How Happy Is' series, says the secret to happiness is knowing you are already happy. You can bring happiness into your mind right now just by choosing to and by using your wonderful imagination.

Here's another exercise based on what we already do. It's no mistake that nature has naturally given us the ability to sigh. This is often an automatic reaction when we are looking for that little bit more within us to carry on with what we either want or need to do. Now you can use this natural ability to maximum effect with the following exercise.

Exercise

Power Breaths

This quick and easy technique boosts your focus, calms you down and brings you into the now, all in 3 breaths! Added to that you can use it anytime, anywhere. This is an important technique as part of the ChapWell Method and so easy to do.

1. Get yourself in a comfortable, safe place and relax your shoulders. A quick way to do this is to tense and lift your shoulders up as close to your ears as you can whilst drawing in a breath. Then, as you breathe out, let your shoulders drop. Then drop them just a little bit more as you release the last of your breath.

2. Now close your eyes or stare at a fixed point and focus on your breathing.

3. Put your hands on your tummy to feel the rise and fall of your tummy as you breathe.

4. Take a deep breath to a slow count of 1, 2, 3 and pause. Now release your breath slowly to a count of 3, 2, 1 and pause.

5. Repeat this breath 2 more times.

6. Now open your eyes, or look around you if you have chosen to just stare at a fixed point. Come back to the present. Make sure you are fully alert before you carry on with your day. Look at your surroundings afresh and allow your focus to come back to your day or task.

Use this exercise to give yourself a boost or when you are feeling stressed or any other emotion that is bringing you down. One of my course delegates reported she used this exercise whenever a work colleague, whom she found difficult, irritated her. She found her irritation reduced and it gave her a choice about how to respond. Her time at work improved and so did her relationship with her work colleague. Power Breaths are a simple yet effective technique, which brings us great benefits. Now, maybe, you are starting to see the possibilities for you, your life now and all your future nows!

No perfects please

Each exercise in this book is laid out for you with easy steps to follow. At the beginning of each exercise I give you the key points of the exercise so that you know the direction you are going in. You can create your unique approach to each exercise just by following the key steps. Sometimes, after an exercise, clients say something like – *'I'm not sure I did that right as I decided to turn my 10 step staircase into a slope which is easier for me and I started to try and turn it back into a staircase but I did relax, I think'*. The main point is to go deeper into your mind, relax the conscious mind and work through the subconscious. If a downward slope works for you, that's fine; you are going down in your own unique way. Trust your mind to give you what you need. Another client said it was frightening as she found herself in a dark and dingy place. I explained that it is only a thought and she has a perfect opportunity to direct her thoughts. So I advised her to imagine herself easily doing whatever was needed to brighten things up. Next time she got a pot of yellow sunshine and painted all the walls with it! She now calls the 'Comfy Chair Exercise' her sunshine trip!

Get ready for action

This book is not a theory-packed book – it is an action-packed book! Yes, there are quick and slightly longer explanations where needed. At the back I have put together a list of books you may find really useful if, like me, you enjoy the theory as much as the practical. My focus is on YOU and putting you in a position to be the lion in your life, to create YOUR life to suit just YOU and your jungle.

As the ChapWell Method draws from many talking and mind therapies, I see myself as just the chef of the dish called the ChapWell Method. I really like to think that somewhere there is a land called ChapWell Land populated with ChapWellians who practise the method and live a totally different life to our modern day life. Therefore I also include some of their sayings, laws and stories to help you enjoy the wonderful power of the ChapWell Method and hopefully develop your understanding too.

Self-study

To support these aims I have designed this book to help you to access the ChapWell Method through self-study or as ongoing support following attending a course or one-to-one coaching with me. You choose what suits you best; it's your lion and your jungle!

Begin your wonderful journey

No need to pack, just open your mind to releasing your power using the ChapWell Method and get ready to bring relaxation, calm and peace into your life. When you check in you can begin to easily and effortlessly create your happiness, success and wellbeing.

The Tale of the Three Lions

A long time ago in ChapWell Land a large group of lions and lionesses roamed freely in the jungle. They had three leaders, one called Peace, another named Calm and a third known as Focus. This group lived a settled life; they hunted, had families, enjoyed the jungle that surrounded them and thrived.

Then one day a great drought came upon the land and all the other animals began to migrate to find land with better water sources.

The three lion leaders recognised that food was getting short, as more and more time was spent hunting for little or no return. Families no longer thrived, with young and old becoming ill, and constant arguments breaking out amongst the lions.

Peace was very worried about this and constantly urged the lions and lionesses to look after each other in these hard times. Meanwhile Calm urged everyone to relax and try and enjoy this time as it too would pass; yes it was hard, but Calm urged them to remember that nothing lasts for ever.

To this one young lion, called Free, replied, 'That's all very well for you to say, but if we don't help ourselves and move to a better place, free of the drought and with plenty of food, we will find out it's we who don't last forever!'

Focus stepped forward and thanked Free for his clear commentary on the situation. 'It seems we have a choice of actions: do nothing, wait and see what happens, or debate the issue to find a suitable course of action and continue to argue about it, which is probably the same as our first course of action. I agree none of these seem hopeful, possible, but not hopeful. However, there is always another option'

Then all three leaders looked at the crowd, waited a moment and then, slowly, together they turned towards the road ... and a new direction, as yet not taken.

Chapter 2
Dump the Stress, Select Success

Key 1: A focused and peaceful mind

A peaceful mind is a powerful mind. A powerful mind is a focused mind. A focused mind is a creative mind. A creative mind is a successful mind. A successful mind creates a successful life, wellbeing and happiness.

ChapWellian Guidance Section 9, paragragh 23

Do you wake up in the morning knowing you'll feel confident, calm and peaceful today no matter what happens?

Do you know if you can trust yourself to take you safely through whatever the day brings?

Do you want to

- Kick stress, anxiety and worry right out of your life?
- Enjoy a relaxed, calm and peaceful approach to your days?
- Sleep peacefully and wake feeling restored and re-freshed?
- Easily manage your days and all they bring?

With these 7 keys you have everything you need to live your life in a state of happiness and wellbeing; you just need to use the first Key and then pick and choose your way to using the other 6 keys in this book. Would you believe me if I then said, 'These keys were designed so they fit the lock to the cage you sit in, allow you to stroll out and live the life you maybe wish you had the confidence to create.' I wonder what you would do? Would you pounce like the lion or scurry away like the mouse?

Here is a bit more about those **7 keys** that make up the **ChapWell Method.**

- Key 1 – Create a focused, peaceful mind
- Key 2 – Living in the now
- Key 3 – Turbo-boost your Power - Clear out those negative thoughts, calm the chatter of the mind and install positive, nurturing thoughts
- Key 4 – Your inner wisdom - Get to **really** know yourself, trust yourself and tap into your inner knowing and talents
- Key 5 – Use now to create your nows - Create and install new strategies and programmes to suit you and your jungle
- Key 6 – Feed your need mores - Choose and create the future you want
- Key 7 – Sweep aside the barriers - Simply unlock your cage and release your fears

Easy tools for the uniqueness of your jungle

The 7 keys allow your wonderful mind to create exactly what you need and want to include effortlessly in your life.

First you start with Key 1, your Master Key, which allows you to direct your powerful mind to support you, build you up AND, most importantly, feel the benefits from your very first exercise.

1 plus 6

The first key allows you to relax and start working with your mind to create your jungle, your happiness, success and wellbeing, easily creating the life that you want. If life is a jungle, who do you want to be, the lion or the mouse? Before I appear to be anti-mice I should say, please feel free to choose to be the mouse, but just make sure your mouse is happy, thriving and not shivering in a cage!

Each key includes simple tools to free your mind from thinking patterns and habits that are pulling you away from your life well lived. The important thing is that you must install something in its place and that something is what you want to create, be, think or feel. This is important, because otherwise you will leave a gap that will be filled by something you maybe don't want or more of what you already have and don't want!

So back to that first key which shows you how to effortlessly use self-hypnosis and relaxation to tap into your wonderful power and imagination.

Why relaxation and calm?

Think about it: I believe our biggest struggle these days is to manage the stress, pressure, demands or whatever you want to call it of our everyday lives. All our energy can easily be poured into keeping up, staying on top, and striving for success in this modern day world. This is what I call the jungle of life.

If you have ever been to a jungle you will know they are glorious places to travel in when you have the right tools, equipment and guide. However, without the right equipment, guide and tools, jungles can be frightening, dangerous places. Somewhere where you have to be constantly on your guard against unknown, unpredictable dangers. A tense, frightening place with no time or space to enjoy the beauty, life force and wonders of the jungle. Now I wonder how you want to travel through your jungle: as a lion, striding through, hunting, resting, eating, playing when you feel the need, or shivering, giving up, or worse, fighting like a frightened, caged lion? I just wonder what would you choose for your jungle journey?

So it makes sense that anything to help us find a way to relax and experience calm whilst building us up has got to be a better approach. It's no mistake that the optimum state for learning, focus, achievement and alertness can be achieved by having a relaxed and peaceful mind. Knowing all of this, why do so many of us choose stressful states to make ourselves perform? By this I mean criticising our efforts, telling ourselves to do better, that we are not good enough, piling on the stress and threats and expecting ourselves to perform expertly and happily in our life.
It is important to approach these exercises in a light hearted way, have fun and allow your mind to use your wonderful imagination. Remember my comment earlier: if what your mind gives you doesn't suit, just change it; it's your mind and you are in charge. Allow your wonderful imagination to

do the work for you, remembering that if you can imagine it then you can create it!

Not much imagination?

A client once said to me that she did not have much imagination so doubted the exercises would work for her. When I asked her if she worried, quick as a flash she said she was born a worrier, adding that she seemed to be getting worse as she got older. I then explained that worry was her imagination working hard. I explained that to worry you need to be thinking what if..., how am I going to... and so on, imagining all the scenarios that actually haven't happened yet! That's your imagination hard at work and you believe it because you worry, stress, work harder to make sure something doesn't happen that actually is only in your imagination. It's that powerful, though, as it's got you doing all sorts of things just in case! I find that people, like me (once), who worry have the greatest capacity to create wonderful changes in their life. They simply need to change the strategy, learnt long ago, of journeying through their jungle planning and defending against the worst. Just imagine if all that worry energy went into creating what you want; how would you feel, and what would you dare to want?

As children we daydream, we create and imagine. Sadly, as we grow and mature, we are told there are more important things, life becomes too busy and we become human doings rather than human beings. The techniques you will use work with your imagination, allowing it to grow and flourish to build up and make powerful strides through your jungle to all the good things you deserve.

The ChapWell Method also works with that wonderful and accepted law of attraction: the more you focus on what you want, the more you can start creating it consciously and powerfully subconsciously! A winning combination! Your mind so wants to work powerfully for you and all you need to do is direct it and simply show it how.

Don't overthink, just do the work and enjoy the wonderful results

Learn to accept whatever your mind gives in the exercises as symbolic for you; don't bother analysing or overthinking the images or representations your imagination gives you. They just mean what you direct them to mean. Your unique mind will understand totally. Frequently I work with people who, over time, have developed many skills and the knowledge to develop themselves. However they often analyse things, critique each of their experiences and justify them using their understanding, knowledge and skills. The trouble with doing this is you become an observer in your life and experience and spend too much time interpreting what is happening rather than just changing it to suit you and enjoying life. Focus on what you want, not what you want to lose; stop analysing is my advice. Forget justifying your thoughts, feelings and emotions; at the most all you get is more of what you don't want or, worse still, you become a human observer and your life is the experiment!

Key 1 Create a focused, peaceful mind

This key creates relaxation, peace and calm in your mind through self-hypnosis. Your mind is a powerful tool and works for you all of the time. The only trouble is we forget to show or tell it what we want and how we want it to work for us, so we leave it to do the best it can. Problems, stress and frustrations start to build as many of us use old thinking patterns often learnt from others and our past. These are ways of thinking designed for times and people past, and we wonder why we run into the same problems, or just create new ways to struggle.

Learning how to direct your mind equips you to create ways of thinking, feeling and acting to work for your now: new situations, new stages of your life, new challenges and so on. Are you still using old directions and wondering why they don't work for you now? So how do you help yourself out? Through stress, worry and anger or finding new ways? Key 1 is your first step – relaxing and calming your mind so you can start directing your mind to support you and give you what you want. As soon as you turn your first key you can then use your other keys in any order you want! Easy!

> The first way may not be the last way, but the last way will always lead to the next way.
>
> ChapWellian saying circa 1215

Stress, anxiety, worry etc, etc

In this complex, modern world of today we don't regularly come across life-threatening situations. I believe we experience 'ego threatening' situations which trigger our fight/flight reflex, causing a stress reaction in our bodies much more frequently than our bodies and minds were designed to tolerate. Maybe our biggest predator is now in our minds and how we interpret the world about us! No matter if it is right or wrong. Research and my practice have shown that a great many of us are experiencing levels of stress today at a higher rate than is good for us. Stress can be a good thing; it releases adrenaline, preparing the mind and body to be able to perform at our peak levels. However, if it is too frequently triggered, swamping the body with adrenaline, putting our systems on high alert for too long, it chips away at our wellbeing and peace of mind and can then impact negatively on our physical and mental health.

You need to nurture and feed your mind to allow it to perform excellently. We all know the body needs a good nutritious diet and regular exercise to remain in good condition. So these exercises are your workout for the mind, to allow you to relax and recharge and for your mind to work brilliantly for you, as you direct it to give you what you want.

Consider athletes. They do not perform at their peak abilities for the race all of the time. Rather they work on maintaining and building up their physical and mental strength to be able to perform at their absolute maximum when they need to. They do this through training, rest and nourishing their bodies and minds. So why don't we approach our lives like that? Why do so many of us run on adrenaline triggered by stress for too long and too frequently, and how can we expect to experience happiness, wellbeing and enjoy our life?

Key 1 gives you the rich training ground for your success

whilst building you up from the first exercise you do. It builds your ability to relax your conscious mind which then allows you to work with your subconscious mind where the firmly installed old ways of doing things are held. It allows you to easily and effortlessly choose new ways of thinking that work for you now, strengthen you and make your happiness, wellbeing and success a reality. By turning the Master Key you set up a trigger or instant pathway to relaxation, peace and calm. Now who wouldn't want that?

Exercise - Key 1 – Comfy Chair Self-Hypnosis

Safety first – before you start just a reminder about safety.

To do this you'll need to find somewhere where you can be by yourself, totally switch off from the outside world safely and ensure no interruptions, phone off, battery out of the doorbell, that sort of thing. Just follow the key points, and remember no perfects are needed. As soon as you start using Key 1 you'll feel the benefits, it's not an exact science so you cannot go wrong, from that first deep breath you are doing it, not trying, just doing. The first time delegates do this on my courses I talk them through and then get them to do it for themselves. The first time I self-hypnotised myself I thought I'd never remember this so opened my eyes when I got stuck and followed through the instructions that way and it worked. So for your first time you can either record the instructions (or you can visit my website, www.

chapwellmethod.com/comfychair, and download a recording of the exercise as an added bonus) or follow the version below, referring to the instructions as you go into a hypnotic state. The very next time, enjoy taking yourself into a hypnotic state by yourself; you will find it easy. Just make sure you are as safe as if you are going to sleep, e.g. lock any doors etc.

Key Points – what to do and remember, absolutely no perfects please!

Relaxing the body

- **Doubling the relaxation from the top of your head to the tip of your toes – relaxing, imagining softening all of your muscles as you go**

- **Walk down a 10 step staircase**

- **Go through a door into your own, special, safe place**

- **Enjoy creating your safe place exactly as you want it**

- **Sit in a comfy chair and feel that wonderful feeling of relaxation whilst you enjoy your safe, special place**

- **Leave your chair when you are ready, go through the door and count yourself up the steps back into the now**

1. Get yourself comfortable, either sitting or lying. Try and make sure your back is straight and supported and your legs and arms are uncrossed. This will ensure you don't 'come to' with pins and needles or a stiff back from an awkward position.

2. Power Breaths – Breathe in counting 1, 2, 3, pause and out 3, 2, 1, pause. Repeat for 3–5 breaths.

3. As you breathe allow your eyes to close or focus on a fixed point directly in front of you.

4. Allow your breathing to settle to normal and let your attention wander down to your feet. Notice how heavy they feel and imagine them feeling heavier in a warm comfy way.

5. Let this warm, comfy feeling of weight travel slowly up your legs. Feel the chair, floor or bed supporting you as your weight starts to sink into that support.

6. Concentrate on moving this heavy feeling all the way up your body, one limb at a time, right up to the top of your head.

7. Now wallow in that wonderful relaxed feeling of total heaviness throughout your body.

8. Now you can easily double that relaxation. Imagine that relaxed feeling of heaviness doubling and flowing down your body from the top of your head. Feel the relaxing weight spread around your eyes, cheeks and mouth.

9. Imagine the heaviness working its way down your back whilst relaxing all of the muscles in your neck and back.

10. Continue to travel in your mind increasing the relaxing heaviness in each part of your body until you reach your toes.

11. Feel yourself sinking into the chair, bed or floor so that your weight is fully supported.

12. Now imagine walking down a 10 step staircase; count each step as you go down to the bottom. The staircase can be exactly as you want it; it's your staircase so enjoy going down the 10 steps!

13. At the bottom of the stairs is a door. Open the door and go into the room or place. Sink into a lovely comfy chair and look around your room or maybe it's an outside space or a summer house. Just enjoy whatever your mind gives you and change anything that doesn't suit to exactly how you want it. This is your room, your place; you can make it look however you want. Choose your favourite colours, pictures, rugs, music

playing, or if outside, choose the landscape to suit you. Enjoy creating this peaceful oasis as you sink into your comfy chair.

14. Relax and stay for as long as you want, enjoying the peace and calm of your unique space all the time relaxing in your comfy chair. When you are ready to come back into the now, get up from your comfy chair; take one last look at your chair so you will recognise it later.

15. Walk through the door to your staircase. Walk up the stairs counting each step, from 10 to 1, the top step.

16. Open your eyes and stretch. Give yourself enough time to come back into the now, just as if you had been asleep.

Do this exercise as often as you can over the next week. On my courses I suggest you do it just before you go to sleep every night or most nights until your 'mini relax and peace comfy chair' is fully charged for you to tap into a quick peace and relaxation recharge. If you are doing the exercise just before you go to sleep, leave out bringing yourself back to the now and just stay in your comfy chair. Most people on my courses find this helps them sleep more peacefully too.

Practise tapping into your store of peace and calm during the day. When you have a minute, imagine yourself back in your comfy chair and feel that beautiful feeling of relaxation and peace as you mentally sink into your comfy chair. In truth most people experience a feeling of peace and relaxation by thinking of their comfy chair after their very first self-hypnosis experience. By repeating the Comfy Chair Exercise a few times you are simply boosting the strength of that peaceful and calm feeling linked to your comfy chair. Just like the happiness exercise in Chapter 1, you are now building up a pathway to a peace and relaxation store.

Once you have fully charged your 'Comfy Chair' you can trigger peace and relaxation in yourself in two ways. One, as you go about your day and just imagine yourself, for a moment, a thought, in the comfy chair, that feeling of peace and calm will flow through your body. If you have a little more time, say 5 to 10 minutes, or are feeling particularly challenged, use the Mini Relax to really wallow in peace, calm and relaxation. Give yourself a boost and reset yourself to a state of peace, calm and relaxation.

Exercise - Mini Relax and Comfy Chair

As usual make sure you are safe to 'switch off' from the outside world for a few minutes.

1. Make yourself comfortable.

2. Power Breaths – using your 3 breaths to relax yourself. Breathe in counting 1, 2, 3, pause and out 3, 2, 1 pause.

3. Allow your breathing to gently return to its normal rhythm.

4. Imagine yourself in your comfy chair in your special place. Enjoy that feeling of relaxation, peace and calm as it flows through you.

5. Feel your body relaxing deeper into your chair and for a few moments enjoy looking around, being in your safe, special place.

6. When you are ready to return notice your breathing and gradually come back to the now.

7. Stretch, yawn, blink and bring yourself fully back into the here and now before you start doing anything. Treat yourself the same as if you have just woken up; don't go dashing around until you are fully awake.

I use this mini booster throughout the day, especially when I am having a busy day or am feeling in need of a rest but it's just not possible at that point. I sometimes spend a minute in my 'virtual chair' just before I switch on the car engine and take off to my next appointment. Just remember to stretch and yawn and continue with what you want to get done **only when you are fully alert again**. You have been in a trance and need to make sure you are fully alert before you do anything.

The important thing to understand is that by repeating the longer self-hypnosis Comfy Chair Exercise and visiting your room, you are building up a store place of peace and relaxation that is limitless! It is ready for you to visit without having to fully relax yourself, an essential booster in our busy lives. By just flicking your mind to your chair and being aware of the peace, calm and relaxation you experience, you are setting your trigger or pathway, if you like, to that wonderful feeling. You can then effortlessly trigger your mind into peace, calm and relaxation by just imagining yourself in your comfy chair. Sometimes it takes a few days but very soon you will have provided yourself with your own instant relaxation and peace chair to be summoned at your beck and call. Each time you bring it into your day it becomes more of you and your natural state! Much better than allowing the highs and lows of the day to dictate our wellbeing, happiness and in time our state of health too.

Sad times are sad, disappointments hurt, success lifts, laughter cheers; happiness, joy, love and loss are all a part of life.

So travel with peace and calm as a constant part of you to smooth your way as you travel through life.

ChapWellian Guidance 20:11 circa 0955

The Tale of the Ice Sellers

Although surrounded by water, Chapwell Land is very hot for nine months of the year. So hot that the Chapwellians move to ice houses to live and work. They even have communal ice halls for Chapwellians to sit in, relax, practise the 7 keys or just meet and talk, enjoying the cooling effect of the ice.

Long tunnels, going deep into the mountain's centre, lead to ice pockets and these provide a never- ending supply of ice.

The rights to mine for ice were, long ago, assigned to two families called Icer and Berger.

The two families had worked closely together for hundreds of years. Every morning during the hot season they would travel down the tunnels into the ice pockets, cut the ice and transport it back to the surface using carts.

Other members of the two families would then wrap the ice in special sheets to keep it frozen and cart the ice to wherever it was needed.

As the Chapwellian population grew, more and more ice was needed. The two families worked longer and longer hours, struggling to meet the demand for ice. One day after a particularly long, hard day the heads of the Icer and Berger family, both exhausted, agreed they couldn't go on like this.

Berger insisted they just tell everyone how much ice they could have and that was that! Icer disagreed and pointed out that it was their responsibility to bring ice to all. Both men discussed the possibilities. Berger insisted that they stick with tried and tested processes and carry on doing the best they could. After all no one could ask more than that, could they?

Icer then told him about his dream, where everyone had enough ice, and showed Berger a rough sketch of how he believed it possible to provide enough ice and have enough time for themselves and their families. Berger smiled and agreed that would be the best solution but it was just a dream.

Icer laughed and said he believed in dreams, after all, dreams are the first step to reality, aren't they? Berger joined in the laughter, replying, 'If you want to spend your precious holiday time on dreams that is up to you. Me, I'm going to rest and build up my strength so I can cope with the next ice season,' adding that Icer should do the same.

Laughter turned to discussion and discussion turned to argument as the two men tried to agree a solution. Berger was convinced it was the Chapwellians' fault and they needed to be made to restrict their ice use, whilst Icer insisted they were responsible for providing ice and needed to find a way to suit themselves to do that.

Sadly the men could not agree and the argument escalated. In the end it was decided the only way to settle things was to separate the mines, each family running their own mine.

Icer spent all of his holiday time working on his dream machine whilst Berger rested, warning Icer he would not survive the next ice season if he didn't rest. People began to whisper that Icer had lost his mind and spent every moment locked in his shed talking of dreams and frozen sheds.

As the next ice season began, both families worked the mines separately. Again Berger and his family worked all hours and days possible, only stopping to eat and sleep. As Berger walked to his mine he saw Icer and his family sitting down outside their mine looking relaxed and happy. In the background he could hear weird clunking noises.

Icer saw Berger approach and invited him in to see his dream. Berger was amazed as he walked through the sheds stacked high with ice, none of it melting, while a hole in the wall churned out ice blocks ready to stack.

Berger spoke first and congratulated his friend on his success. Icer thanked him and explained the whole process and invited him to rejoin the two mines. Berger looked at him suspiciously. 'Why would you do that now?' he asked. 'My success is not your failure. I have time to be generous,' he replied.

Chapter 3
The Power of Now

Key 2 – Living in the now!

> A bright young scholar once asked his teacher what was so important about living in the now. And his teacher replied that he was too busy to answer such a simple question.
>
> ChapWellian Saying circa 905

What would you do now if you knew you could trust yourself to cope with whatever life gives you, good and bad?

Do you know how to live and stay in the now?

Where do you live, where are your thoughts? In the now, the past or the future?

Do you choose to give away the power of now?

Your second key – living in the now

Key 2 shows you how to live in the now and enjoy boosting your future nows. Living in the now sounds simple but so often we get caught up in what's next, removing our focus and engagement with what is happening now. This brings us down as we unwittingly take away our natural-born need to enjoy what we are doing now. Yes, I believe it is a natural-born need to feel happy now, to enjoy our now, yet we frequently deny ourselves, always thinking beyond what's happening now. What did she/he mean by that? What's going on here? What might happen? What might go wrong, what might work, and on and on.

Often we are too busy trying to finish what we are doing and all the time focusing on the next thing, the future, something that's not happening yet! In so doing we take away or limit our life experience and with it limit our chances to experience enjoyment, contentment or at least feel OK.

Think about it: if you are letting your mind wander elsewhere, when do you get to live the life you have now? Worse still, we are putting our minds to situations that haven't yet happened, and may not even happen. So whose life are you living? A real one or a 'might' one?

Do you recognise any of these thoughts – 'I must keep an eye on the time otherwise I am going to be late', 'I wonder if he'll like my report', 'What did he/she mean when s/he said that?', 'I wonder if I can get that done before I get...', 'Perhaps if I pick it up before I go to...', 'I hope it is all going OK and what if ...' and so on. I'm pretty sure even if I haven't repeated your exact thoughts you get the general idea and can also match the general trend with some of your thoughts.

If you need to plan your day to go smoothly, plan it. Whilst planning your day, week, month, year, enjoy the process of planning, sorting and organising. When my husband got sick and the outlook was not good I had to learn how to enjoy the now as that was all we knew we had. Don't wait until you are in a situation that teaches you this lesson, start now. Now is all we truly have anyway. Being someone that naturally looked ahead and planned ahead, having to live day by day, moment by moment, came very hard. That's when I started developing these tools to enjoy the now even if I'd only had a few hours' sleep in the past 48 hours. Incidentally, they do say that one hour's hypnosis is akin to eight hours asleep and I do believe it's true! Only as a short term solution though!

To recap, using your comfy chair you can bring peace, calm and a wonderful feeling of relaxation into your 'now' as you go about your day. Draw on it frequently to enable you to enjoy the now and focus exactly on what you are doing, just being, moment by moment. Don't forget too to use your happiness well from Chapter 1 and your 3 breaths as constant supportive tools. They are part of your toolkit for the jungle, so practise them and enjoy the benefits; there's no need to wait.

Lost in the now!

I have developed the ability to totally focus, be in the now, so strongly I suddenly realised that I was losing track of time. Just like you do when you are having a good time, time flies by. Regardless of what I was doing, whether work, mundane chores or play, that sense of satisfaction increased my awareness of just doing and, importantly, just being was given back to me. I say 'doing'; don't pick me up on it – I live in the real world and I'm also someone who likes to do a lot of things but I am able to BE me and in the now, whilst I get everything done that I need to get done. (You'll also find me wandering off into the future, enjoying planning in the now, taking small steps towards my goals; we don't have to be perfect, just ourselves, living in the now.) Somehow, and this is the case in many other practices such as mindfulness and meditation, time seems to expand and I truly feel like I have more time!

Forget the time and let time support you

Anyway, back to this getting in the now. If you are someone who needs to keep a close check on the time, keep appointments, collect children and so on, just start using modern technology to help you stay in the now in your life. Set the alarm on your phone or watch, or carry a mini alarm, whatever you have, and then you can safely relax into what you are doing now without bashing yourself over the head with the 'What time is it?' syndrome. Remember that our habit of looking ahead, thinking about, and maybe even fretting about the next thing we have to do is robbing us of our now moments. In short we are always living in the future or the past when the only thing we really have is now! Yes, revisiting a past happy memory is good, and remembering a past sad event or person to find your peace within that time, event, loss, or disappointment is good and helps us find acceptance (more about that later in Chapter 9). But for now you are learning about living in the now and staying in the now. The more you are in the now the more you can discern what you need to focus your attention on.

Get real about time

The nature of me and my work means that I tend to have several things on the go and those things have deadlines and timelines always agreed with me or by me. The trouble was I was frequently underestimating how long those jobs took me to do and this resulted in me, being a very reliable little soul, working for far too long into what should have been my playtime! I have met and worked with many people, like me, running what I call an anti-playtime programme!

Living in the now and setting my phone alarm helped me get a realistic record of how long it takes me to do things. I'm sure you've worked it out; I started keeping a record of my probable timings for certain tasks and I was able to start controlling my workload. In my time log I also include things that must happen for me such as walking and freshly laundered clothes. I'm not saying they don't matter; they do to me and I know how much time I need to make sure they are in place and NOT rushed! I am really meeting my needs. How are you meeting all your needs? Do you really know what your needs are?

'To do lists' or 'not to finish lists' or 'beat yourself up lists' – which do you use?

Which do you create? This simple trick helps you to find your way through the pile and also to avoid distractions unless you choose to be distracted, of course! First get the things you have to get done that day out of your head, as well as the things you'd like to do. What are they doing in your head? Maybe stopping you being you! My favourite way is to use post-its. This really helps you get that balance too.

Exercise – Post-it

Use two colours of post-its, one colour for the 'must do things', those activities where you are giving out, and one colour for the 'I'd like to do things' where you are allowing yourself to get something back from life, recharging through doing the things you really enjoy (I'm talking fun things here that recharge your batteries). Put one thing per post-it, remembering to use different colours for 'must do' and 'want to do'. Spread all the post-its on a table top, shelf or wherever you can see them clearly and they can stay.

At a glance you can see how many 'want to do' and 'must do' post-its you have. Is there a fair split, a balance between the two colours, or is there a very one-sided split? Is the balance good for you? On a work day there are going to be more 'must dos' so I tend to go for a 3 to 1 balance, more or less, depending on how big the tasks are. I then put in 'want to do' post-its to make sure I have a balance of giving out and recharging. Start becoming aware of the need to make sure you have some fun, 'want to do' things in there. I'm not talking about big things: for my personal 'want to do' post-its I'll have 5 minutes talking to my older self (Chapter 5) for guidance, or knitting a square for the blanket I am making, 20 minutes gardening, a cup of coffee as I wander around the garden, right next to the finish report post-its, prepare for client, outline magazine article etc. Now as you finish each 'to do' thing just pick up the post-it and throw it away, leaving a blank space! If you travel around during your day, as I sometimes do, just put your post-its on a sheet of paper and carry that with you.

This simple approach to managing your day, whatever you do, helps you provide some distance, gives you easy feedback on your progress and allows you to focus on what you are doing, in the now.

If I come across something for another day, I carry post-its with me and just write it on them for another day. So the next day I have some post-its to start with, perhaps what didn't get done yesterday and whatever I have already put on my post-its. I also store those 'next day' post-its in my diary, sticking them to the day I am going to do them. If a page/day has three work things I know I need to put them on another day, maybe negotiate another deadline or actually turn the work down. Three per day really does make me focus and ensure I have a balance of work and play. This system quickly helps you realise if you have too much going on, and are maybe not boosting yourself with fun things or just things you like doing. It also makes you realise when you have too much on, and maybe you think there is nothing you can do about it. Are you really sure no one can help? When did you last ask? Did you ask? Maybe your fear is keeping you from asking for help and saying no? What if you weren't there to do it tomorrow? What would happen then? Frequently we burden ourselves with things for fear of being found wanting. This is just another bar in our cage. The taking action is critical: talk, negotiate and bring about the changes you need. More about that later.

The unexpected demands – think of the answer and respond

So when planning my workload I stopped getting into those panicked, late-night working situations unnecessarily! Sometimes the unexpected comes up and we're needed by family, friends and colleagues and we decide to help. When I find myself in that situation I now know what I am saying 'Yes' to and can then decide if it is possible, doable and OK with me! Just a quick glance at all my things for today and the question is, 'Have I room for another post-it?' If I do decide there's no room but I want to say yes, the next decision is what 'must do' is going to have to move over to another day? I also know that if I cannot help there will be someone else that can and I'm letting them have their turn! After all, it's a bit arrogant to think we are the only ones that can help or do a particular thing, isn't it? Don't you think we should make sure everyone enjoys that pleasure?

Now is now

So let's get some more tools to help us stay in the power of now. We have already discussed the importance of now – it is all we have; the past has gone, unchangeable, and the future hasn't arrived yet. How often do you waste your now by letting your mind run back to the past, chewing over events that you cannot change, or trying to anticipate the future? If you are doing that, here's a great way to clear your mind and firmly direct it into the NOW!

Step by step

Do you know we simply throw away between 3,000 to 5,000 opportunities each day to bring our minds into the now? That's the usual number of steps that we all take each day, just going from there to here and back to there. Start watching people as they walk, and notice how they often walk with their heads down, probably using the time to worry, think about all the things they need to do, anything other than enjoying the walk, the weather, just being in the world. It's so easy to clear our minds, give ourselves a rest and just 'be' and, as we go about our day, keep ourselves firmly placed in the now! Each step can enable us to simply focus on our now and enjoy just being.

Not just walking

If you use a chair or other device to get you around I have it on good authority you can still do these exercises any time you move and even when resting. They still work with a bit of modification either by walking in your mind, using the rhythm of your movement or listening to music. (Put some music on and use the rhythm of the music to carry out the activities; that tip came courtesy of my husband when mobility wasn't easy for him.)

The power of NOW Walking

Added to the bonus of being in the now these fun and quirky exercises clear the mind, give it a rest and a refresh, ready to return your focus to whatever your 'now' holds. They are great to clear your mind from one thing to the next, and to clear emotions too, not just thoughts.

Have you ever snapped at the wrong person, and dealt with a situation badly because you were angry or upset by something or someone else? Something that now really belongs in the past, gone, finished, but you cannot quite let it go? You know that feeling when your mind keeps mulling it over, reminding you of how it didn't work out and making you feel bad even though you know it doesn't help? It happens to us all but what would you choose if you had a choice? To lose those unhelpful emotions so that you can deal with your now in a state of peace, calm and wellbeing? Or keep on fretting, feeling hard done by or not good enough? Now Walking gives you a choice to refresh and refocus your mind to peace and calm.

The 'state' you're in

No matter what you are doing and how you are feeling, calm or stressed, you are in a 'state'. That state is made up of three things – actions, feelings and thoughts. Change any one of those and the others will follow. Feel happy and your body and thoughts will follow. Start slumping your body, hunch your shoulders, and your thoughts and feelings follow.

This technique gives you the key to manage your state

and create peace and calm, happiness and wellbeing, an optimum development state for the mind. States that you can choose and use. What would you choose: confidence, energy, focus, happiness, wellbeing or something else? You choose: it's your jungle, your cage and your keys to living the life you choose!

This method works with you, the uniqueness of you and the life you are meant to live! Not my way but your way. The practical, easy tools are designed for anyone to use and create their unique journey, easily tapping into happiness and wellbeing as they journey through life. Maybe I am in danger of repeating this too much, however I truly believe you are the expert on you so giving you the keys enables you to create your unique life to suit you.

Now Walks show you how to simply use your everyday walking to defocus, release negative emotions and refocus on the now and rest your mind. Now Walking gives you an everyday way to boost your peace of mind, be open to what is happening now and is also a brilliant tool to reduce stress and anxiety levels. The walks will break that body surge of adrenaline and stop your mind and emotions feeding it, or your 'ego thinking' making sure you trigger your 'under threat' buttons: worry, worry, stress, stress. I wonder if you know what I am talking about?

A Now Walk a day

You can try all of the Now Walks and maybe there will be one you prefer or you'll draw on all of them, just like I do. Remember they are an easy way to shut down your mind, give it a rest and then allow your thinking to come back into the now in a peaceful state. I suggest that you first try one at a time, starting with the one you are most attracted to and use it as much as you remember and can over the next few days. Then try another for a few days and when you have tried all of them pick your favourites or use them all whenever you need to get yourself into the now or need a boost. The Happiness Walk lifts you right up and helps you to create a lightness of mood very quickly. You choose, and don't forget to choose!

Now Walk 1 – Counting Refresher Walk

I learnt this one years ago so I'm not sure who created it, but my thanks to them anyway and apologies for not asking permission to use or modify it.

First the usual safety reminders. Do not 'Now Walk' when you are in a busy, hazardous area, where you need to stay fully alert for your safety and that of others. Personally, I use this after I finish work and am walking back to my car as it helps me shut down my mind from work and allows me to focus on what I am doing now. It unwinds me after work very quickly. How much of your free time are you using to unwind from work or a past situation? I also use the 'Counting Refresher Walk' during the day walking from the office, to the bathroom, to the kettle or from the training room and so on. When I am out Nordic Walking I use it again so I can really switch off and enjoy being out in nature.

1. You are counting your footsteps in groups of 7 as you walk.

2. Be aware of your foot meeting the floor/ground and count each step – one and so on up to 7 steps.

3. Now here comes the fun bit – when you reach step 7 keep counting starting at 2 and count each step to 8.

4. When you reach step 8 take the next step starting at 3 until you reach 9.

5. Continue counting on each step starting at the next higher number and only counting 7 steps on.

6. **Essential Point – If at any point you get lost, confused or hesitate YOU MUST start again at 1 to 7 and then 2 to 8 and so on.** Not only does this keep your mind busy and focused on walking but it also gives your mind a powerful message: it's OK to make mistakes, I can sort it easily! Mistakes are just a part of life.

7. When you stop walking you will find your mind is free to focus on your 'now'.

8. If you become distracted and your mind starts thinking of other things just gently start at 1 and carry on counting.

And that's it; remember there is no competition in this and no judgements on how good you are at it. Forget judgements and allow yourself to become involved in the process. I haven't managed to get past starting to count at 12 and it really doesn't matter. You will reap the benefits from your first step, keeping your mind occupied and allowing your thoughts to go away and give you a rest! Brilliant!

Now Walk 2 – Awareness Walk

Sorry to keep repeating the safety bit and instructions but they are important and maybe you just started with this walk, which is fine. **Remember** to use these walks only when you don't need 100% concentration on hazards and obstacles. Sometimes it's best to try these walks first in the comfort and familiarity of your home, garden or local park, wherever you are familiar with the layout.

The awareness walk is all about raising your awareness of your body. So often we ignore our body and allow our thoughts and even emotions to take control or precedence over everything else. As I have mentioned before, our thoughts and emotions will be reflected in our body, so this exercise aims to reverse that process, clearing the body of negative emotions and allowing the mind and emotions to follow. In addition, being aware of our body is a major step towards good health and responding to our body's needs which helps us to maintain good health. Remember our state relies on three things: thoughts, emotions and body; change one and the others will follow. Note that you are raising your awareness of how your body feels, not making or passing judgements, just accepting how it feels and getting to know your body.

1. As you walk focus on your body. Starting with your feet, notice how they feel in your socks or footwear. Feel your toes, feel each one, feel the ball of your

foot and your heel; notice how it feels when your foot touches the floor as you take each step. If you find yourself making judgements on how your body part feels just direct your mind to feeling the sensation. By judgements I mean each time you find yourself making a judgement e.g. tension, soreness, hot, cold, gently tune back into the feel of that part of your body and allow your awareness and acceptance of the feeling to grow.

2. Place the same level of awareness on your ankles, then your calves and shins and gradually work your way up your body. Focus on each part of your body, just becoming aware of how it feels as you move. Try not to make judgements on the feelings; forget giving the feelings names and just feel each part of your body as it moves. Instead concentrate on experiencing the sensations of your body as it moves.

3. As you walk try to maintain a steady pace. You will walk slowly at first but most people find as they get used to awareness walking they soon revert back to their usual walking pace. It is a good one to also use when you are on a longer walk at first to give yourself a good chance of getting used to a whole body scan. Allow your mind to travel all over your body, focus on each part and just accept how each part of your body feels.

4. When you reach the top of your head move your attention back down to your feet and start the whole process again. Just be aware of each part

of your body, how it moves and the sensations you feel. With this exercise it doesn't matter how far you get, after all it depends on how far you are walking. Each time you use this way of walking you are building up your self-awareness and becoming more aware of your body.

5. **Essential Point – do not judge or label those sensations and feelings; just accept them. I know I keep telling you that but so often we judge rather than experience and this exercise is all about experiencing and being aware of your body whilst it moves.** It will, at first, be perfectly natural for you to make judgements on what the sensations and feelings are and that's fine. Just gently direct your mind back to the sensations and experience how your body feels.

Now Walk 3 – Soothing Walk

Remember that the safety instructions from the previous walks apply to this exercise too.

1. As you walk imagine a bright, white soothing light all around you, just like an aura. Mine is always sparkly white to soothe but you may find your mind gives you a different colour light to soothe you and that is absolutely fine; enjoy your imagination. For some people they do not 'see' the light but just know it is there and that's fine too.

2. Imagine you can direct this bright soothing light to any part of your body, to soothe and relax any areas

that may feel uncomfortable, tense or just enjoy being soothed.

3. Focus on your body. As with the awareness walk start to scan your body but this time direct your light to wherever you feel a need to soothe. Your choice, your body. Sometimes people decide to just work through their whole body and soothe it all. That's absolutely great as you are now starting to meet your unique needs, in your whole body or just parts; you choose.

4. Start with your feet. Feel your toes, feel each one, feel the ball of your foot and your heel, just as you do with the awareness walk.

5. This time note any places you feel tension, discomfort or maybe want to add soothing light towards as they work so hard for you. Direct your bright soothing light right into the area. Imagine the light soothing, relaxing, boosting and melting away any discomfort. Imagine the feeling of any discomfort dissolving, leaving and disappearing from your body. Allow any tensions to just flow from your body into the ground.

6. Keep moving up and down your body in this way using your soothing light to ease, soothe and relax your body at any points you feel any tension.

7. **Essential Point** – If your mind starts wandering off to decide why that part of your body needs soothing, just gently direct your mind back to applying the bright, soothing light to the area.

The history books are full of what happened in the past, how people and events conspired to make people's lives easier or more challenging.

It follows then that a record of how people felt is unnecessary. Happy or sad, stressed or calm, probably all of those things. It wouldn't change anything. We all know people always come through, no matter how they choose to direct their minds to journey through times.

Besides the only person who would care if they were happy or sad is the person themselves and their footprints have long since faded.

Recorded response made by the Chapwellian Senate during a debate on what to include in the Chapwellian Historical Archives. 1455

Safely change

When we are going through changes and things feel beyond our control this is a really good exercise to boost and remind yourself that ultimately all is well, if you choose. This walk helps you find your centre, who you are, and remove yourself from the things life throws at you, all those curveballs and sometimes more. It allows you to return to the problem, issue or unexpected turn in your life with a fresh mind helping you to find a solution, decide on what next or just accept something and move on with your life.

Those things that happen in life – sadness, unexpected twists and turns, and changes that are beyond our control, even at those times when we were not aware of the implications at the time that we took an action or made a decision – maybe they are 'unfair' things or just 'that's life' things. They are the 'why me' things and the answer is simply, why not you?

We are often in the habit of kidding ourselves that if we worry, keep thinking about things and stress we can change things or maybe it will help us find the answer. All this does is make us feel worse, remind us of how helpless and vulnerable we can be in life, and make us feel unsafe. In truth the only thing we can change and have control over is our reaction to whatever is bothering us. Worry, overthinking, stress or whatever you want to call anything that disrupts your peace of mind, doesn't help the situation and worse, it impedes our ability to make sound, measured decisions on what to do or think next. I expect you've heard this many times before and instead of answering 'But I can't help it', you now have the 7 keys of the ChapWell Method to show you how to 'help it' and make a choice on how you want to experience your life.

Sadness as a part of our life journey

I am not suggesting we start laughing and smiling when things are sad or bad, but whoever said that sadness or bad times need to be lived through in a state of stress? I believe that sometimes things are sad and times are bad, but it is still possible to accept this state and work our way through in a state of peace and calm. If we don't choose peace and calm then we begin to use stress, or denial, or other strategies we may have adopted such as anger and frustration. Rather than solve the problem, these learnt strategies increase our stress levels and its associated adrenaline rush impacts on our wellbeing, our state of mind, our relationships, our physical health and our quality of life.

'Remember there is always someone worse off than you'

I have never understood that phrase; why should I feel better thinking about how someone else is having an even harder time than me? Clients come to me wanting to feel stronger, able and positive about their current situation, and I wonder how well they would do if that really was the answer? How does it help me or you to thrive, thinking it could be worse? I am convinced that the sad, tough times are exactly the time when we need to work harder at improving the quality of our feelings and thoughts and directing our behaviour to support us. I have used these techniques through job loss, home loss, grief, divorce, isolation, 24-hour caring duties and then shared them with others through my work and friendships, and without a doubt, the only way through sadness is most definitely upwards in mood, outlook and hope! I have also realised that when things are going along fine they are useful tools to use and practise to boost my wellbeing and develop them as automatic programmes. I was back at the dentist again, today, a place I used to fear. I suddenly realised that I was eager to get into the chair and have my treatment and looking forward to it. I had used the Comfy Chair to enable me to enjoy peace and calm at the dentist's and now my mind was running a relaxation programme in association with the dentist surgery and treatment. Rather than feeling stressed at the dentist's, I now experienced deep calm and looked forward to a root filling!

The ChapWell Method provides you with a choice and enables you to decide how to direct your mind to manage things so you continue to thrive. You can push the stress buttons or you can surround yourself in peace and calm and booster thoughts. For me, I use the ChapWell Method toolkit to experience calm, peace, relaxation and to constantly remind myself I am safe. True, sometimes we don't listen to ourselves; that's only habit and old ways of thinking, but with persistence I have found we listen up quick! So just a day using at least some of those 3,000 to 5,000 opportunities soon gets the mind back under your directorship ... and that's just a lazy day!

Now Walk 4 – Safety Walk

Again, remember the safety instructions for all the 'Now Walks' and follow them.

1. As you walk become aware of your leg swinging forward and your foot stepping down.

2. As your leg swings forward say either aloud or in your mind 'I am' and as you feel your foot touch the ground say 'safe'. Say each word loudly and clearly either out loud or in your mind. Either works well. By the constant repetition, firmness of your voice and physical reinforcement your subconscious gets the message and accepts it as true.

3. Continue walking, saying 'I am' as you swing your leg and 'safe' as your foot reaches the floor.

4. Continue walking making sure you keep your breathing nice and relaxed, saying 'I am' as your leg moves and 'safe' when you put your foot down.

5. If you find your mind wandering start again but this time say 'safe' as you swing your leg forward and 'I am' as you put your foot down.

6. Each time your mind wanders just start again and switch the wording around.

7. You can also adopt this walk to suit you, maybe to bolster your mood or direct your thoughts in any direction you want. Use it to reinforce your intentions and positive, booster thoughts (Chapter 4) as you apply the keys to your life.

It's OK to be upbeat when down

Experiencing the loss of my husband brought me a wonderful gain: the true friendship of like-minded people who were travelling through the same sad time. Despite the sad time we shared a common bond and realised laughter and fun was still allowed, in fact essential. Frequently those friends and people I have worked with have felt social expectations judge and guide them. That if it's a bad, sad or not a good time you mustn't be seen or heard to be enjoying a moment, your time or a peaceful state of mind. If you do seem happy, calm, and at peace everyone thinks you're over it or it's OK with you what is happening and you don't feel, mind or care or you are so strong you don't need support and help. Sometimes this need for approval or judgement can hamper our ability to cope and continue to thrive, learn and develop. A favourite saying for me these days is, 'It is what it is and if you don't want it what do you want?' My point being that we are all unique and will experience similar life events in our own unique way, the best way for us. The conflict occurs when we apply programming, coping strategies that no longer work for us and do not know how to reprogramme our thinking to positively serve the uniqueness of who we are. So during those toughie times, big and small, or just when I feel my confidence is a bit shaky, I do the safety walk. After all, when working with others and myself the single criteria that comes up when working through unwanted or unasked for change is, 'How does this threaten my safety and will I be able to cope?'.

Now Walk 5 – Happiness Walk

Remember, as usual, to keep yourself safe when doing this. I think this may be my favourite one; it gives me an instant boost of happiness leaving me to return to a feeling of wellbeing in the now.

The day will bring what the day brings and this is a great walk to lift the spirits and boost you. Don't think, just do it, and focus on producing a trail of happiness as you walk. This produces good karma too if you subscribe to that viewpoint! Anyone following you now or later will be walking on a path of happiness stamps. This may sound a bit weird but it works and that's all you need.

1. Start walking as if you are really happy; bounce a little as your feet hit the floor.

2. Imagine feeling really happy and walk with a slight bounce. As your feet touch the ground imagine you are stamping happy things on the ground.

3. As your foot goes down imagine you are printing smiles, first step, then chuckles, your second step, then happiness, your third step, in bright colours on the floor or pavement as you go. How that looks is up to you. For me it's like a rainbow trail of happiness streaming out behind me.

4. Keep repeating these happy words in your mind as each foot meets the ground. 3 steps equals 3 words – Smiles, Chuckles and Happiness. You can choose to change smiles and chuckles to whatever words mean happiness for you. So enjoy making this your unique happy walk.

5. Every now and then allow your mind to imagine the trail of happiness you are leaving behind you. Feel good about the happiness anyone who follows your route will also be able, unwittingly, to experience.

6. This walk is great for lifting the spirits and bringing into your mind, body and emotions a wonderful feeling of happiness.

7. **Essential Point** – Be prepared for people to start smiling back at you, as you will find a big grin will soon appear on your face.

I hope you enjoy these wonderful yet simple walking, moving tools to help reset your mind back into the now. When you stop walking you can then focus on the now, bringing with you a feeling of wellbeing.

I was watching a certain programme on TV the other day, that I find very entertaining but there is no way it could be classified as highbrow or educational. I admit that in certain company I wouldn't admit to watching it! Says a lot about me! Anyway I learnt a great big lesson by watching that programme – in just a couple of sentences. A man and a woman were having a conversation to see if they wanted to date. They were talking about the books they had read and the woman mentioned Ekhart Tolle's book *A New Earth*. A book I had read which switched on a million light bulbs for me, if you get my meaning. The man then asked what the book was about. She seemed to fidget and then admitted she hadn't got far with it yet as it was very heavy stuff, and progress was slow. I immediately thought she had just said that to impress and got caught out! Followed by, what a pity, you must read it, it's easy, simple but brilliant. But then I thought that's a judgement, my judgement, as we all find our own way at the right time and pace for us. Haven't I got loads of books hanging around my bookshelves that I want to read, think I ought to read, but somehow haven't found the time for yet?

It made me think that every time we start to move forward and develop, we first need to feel a lack, a desire for something more. Picking the right something more is the important thing and sometimes we need to try a few things to find the thing we need. That's what she was doing, taking first steps, just looking before deciding. So as you work your way through this book and these exercises, just be sure you do it your way. My guidance to start with the Master Key is based on developing the skills of self-hypnosis to accelerate your progress. However, if you want to start with these walks or other exercises then please, ignore my guidance and find your own way into the ChapWell Method, and peace and calm, happiness and wellbeing.

I repeat again – you are unique and can develop these tools at your pace, to suit the wonderful uniqueness of you. This is your journey not mine!

Just a reminder – use your other tools too!

Don't forget to use **Power Breaths** (Chapter 1) too. This handy tool will help you cut through your distracting thoughts and bring your focus back to now! As easy as 3 deep breaths, and easy to do, anytime, anywhere.

Strengthen your comfy chair as a source of peace and calm most nights just before you go to sleep. Visit your comfy chair throughout the day to help you remain centred and surround your day, whatever is happening, with peace and calm.

Living in the now

Start to become aware of your thoughts, just aware of them. Just for a moment reflect on your thoughts: are they really about what is happening, what you are doing, what you want; do they boost you up or pull you down? Or are they all sorts of things and very little related to the now and to what is happening in the now? I wonder if they are related to some past hurt, or maybe a negative thought pattern, some interminable problem, some situation that concerns you or just keeps recurring, just different people, different time? The next exercise shows you how to install a permanent guard to clear away your thoughts and stay in the now!

Exercise – Calm the Chatter of Your Mind

Once you have installed your 'thought guard' you can easily summon it up to clear your mind, whenever you want. By clearing your mind you can redirect your thoughts to support you in the now and be fully present in the now. It takes a bit of practice but as with all these exercises you start to feel the benefits from the very first exercise and your mind will give you everything you need! Call on your guard anytime you want to clear away what I call 'the chatter of the mind'.

Safety first – get yourself in a comfy position where it is safe for you to go inside your mind. This exercise takes about 10–15 minutes to do.

Key points of the exercise

- Relax into your 'comfy chair' in your safe place (Key 1).

- Create your 'mind guard' in detail.

- Give your guard his lifelong duties – to clear your mind.

- Ask your guard for a demonstration.

- Return to your 'comfy chair' place and enjoy the peace and calm.

- Return to the now.

By now I hope you are feeling confident about your ability to self-hypnotise yourself and take yourself into trance just by returning to your 'safe comfy chair place'. So just read through the instructions and create your 'mind guard'. You can use these instructions to refer to during the exercise and just take yourself back into trance quickly and easily by returning to your 'comfy chair place'.

1. Get yourself comfortable and in a safe place where you can go inwards without being disturbed for about 10 to 15 minutes.

2. Power Breaths – Take 3 deep breaths and then allow your breathing to settle to normal.

3. Return to your safe place and sink into your 'comfy chair'.

4. Imagine a friendly guard that sits in your mind; this guard is on your side and will not tolerate anything that doesn't bring out the best in you.

5. Imagine what your guard looks like, his/her/its nose, eyes, body etc. Spend time creating and getting to know your guard, every detail about him/her/it. Notice if your guard is tall/short/round/thin/square/dark/fair and so on. You may find his/her/its name comes into your mind too.

6. Now imagine the armour or clothes s/he/it is wearing. Imagine the colours, the textures, does the armour or clothes make a sound when s/he moves, does it fit tightly or is it loose?

7. Now have a conversation with your guard, introduce yourself, explain this is your mind and give him/her/it their lifelong duties – to clear your mind of thoughts when you give the instruction. Give your instructions in your own words.

8. Hear/see or feel your guard agree and promise to follow your instructions.

9. Now allow your guard to show you how he will grab and dispose of your thoughts so they are completely gone, and your mind is clear and blank. Imagine watching, following or just hearing the guard at work.

10. When you are satisfied your guard is in place and you are confident your guard works how you want them to forever, return to your safe place and enjoy sitting in your comfy chair.

11. When you are ready come back into the now. When you are fully alert you can carry on with your day.

12. Over the next few days regularly call on your guard to clear your mind. Do this as you go about your day; take a minute every now and then to clear your mind using your guard. Just practise this as you go about your day especially if you catch your-self thinking or feeling any negative thoughts.

By repeating over the next few days you are firming up your new programme to calm your mind and clear away unhelpful thoughts. Soon it will become an automatic habit, deeply placed in the subconscious.

Mine is so firmly entrenched now that if I am aware of it at all, I occasionally hear the trap door slam (that's how my guard disposes of the clutter in my mind). Then I realise I was worrying or letting fear-based thinking creep in. Or at least I think I was as my guard grabbed it before it could truly surface to my conscious mind and impact on what I was doing! We have wobbles when our confidence decides to hear, see or feel what I call the confidence dasher, real or imagined. I wonder if you know what I mean. I can be told by 20 delegates how interesting and helpful they find my work but one person will say something negative and I will choose to focus and mull over that one comment! We all know it's best to ignore the naysayer or at best listen, make any necessary adaptations that may be helpful and then forget it! Move on!

Guard your mind and use your guard, as yours
is yours alone unless you choose otherwise!

ChapWellian saying Circa 1450

Remember to allow your mind to give you whatever it wants for your guard; so long as you are comfortable with your guard, keep it. If not, change it. Simply make sure you spend time properly creating and recognising all the little details about him/her/it. Imagine you were asked to identify your guard in an identity parade of similar guards; make sure you can easily recognise your personal mind guard. Previous clients have used the following:

- A floating super powered vacuum cleaner, grey with yellow stripes, that just hung around and sucked up any rubbish; occasionally it burped!

- A witch's broom with eyes and a big, toothless grin, to swish the thought away.

- A flame thrower that burnt any thoughts and blew away the ashes.

You choose or create your own and just let your mind provide you with the best disposal system for you; you'll probably be surprised what your mind creates. The important thing to remember when doing the exercise is to spend your time really creating your guard and being easily able to recognise your guide.

Can't now becomes can!

Already you have some really helpful and life changing tools for your journey through the jungle of life. Are you beginning to travel outside your cage yet, I wonder? So often clients say they don't know how to calm their minds or to relax and that is because they just haven't learnt how to yet! Now **YOU** can, just by a thought, a step or a breath, take action to keep yourself living in the now, surround yourself with peace and calm and clear your thoughts. Remember the more you use techniques the stronger they become, the more automatic the response from your mind, building you up rather than pulling you down. The exercises are a workout for the mind that pays you back straight away; now who wouldn't want that?

The Apprentice and the Master

Chapwellian Tale frequently told to young children when they start judging rather than simply learning and creating.

A talented young apprentice became more and more frustrated with himself as he couldn't produce the beautifully turned table legs he saw his master produce. And quickly he started to dread the time of the day when the apprentices gathered around the master craftsman to be shown another technique which they could practise and learn. Gradually the apprentice's frustrations began to show in his work.

Making more mistakes than usual, his attitude towards his work became blasé and he frequently criticised the newer apprentices.

One day, after the master had watched him arguing with another apprentice, he called the young man into his office. The master asked just one question: 'Do you still want to be a master craftsman?' The apprentice replied, 'Not anymore.' 'Right, you can leave. But first you must share with me your thinking. Those thoughts that helped you decide this, that's all you need do. Then you are free to leave.'

The apprentice explained the wood no longer did what he needed it to do, so what was the point. The master nodded and then asked the apprentice, 'When did you learn all there is to know about working with wood?' The boy looked at him, puzzled, and the master added, 'Because I too would like to know everything about wood rather than accept what each piece of wood gives me and find out how I can use it to create something more.'

Chapter 4
Install Your Power

Key 3 – Turbo-boost your power

Now you have a choice! Keep using negative, critical thinking patterns and just keep clearing them away or choose to take the next step: to become the director of your mind and install positive, power-boosting thoughts to enrich your now and nurture your future nows. This means using your nows and focusing on your nows to create the life you choose.

So now that you can get rid of the chatter in your mind, fill your mind with peace and calm and help your mind to focus on the now using either breath or walking, or both. You can also bring peace and calm into your mind by the summoning of your comfy chair and create a feeling of happiness by drawing on your pool of happy memories.

Learn to create and daydream

Why do you think the lion rests and lolls around a lot? I like to think he is content to just be or maybe he's daydreaming his way to his next success! Yes, you can now dust off that long ago tool, daydreaming (a form of self-hypnosis), and use it to boost and power up your good self. It's official; daydreaming is good for you. You can use it to clear out those negative thought patterns, patterns that help you create the negative thoughts and worries, and instead develop strong positive thought habits. You will be choosing thoughts that support you, enabling you to travel through the jungle of life, living your life confidently, sure of who you are and your right to be there, just like the lion.

Round in circles OK for you?

Now you can remain in peace and calm and clear your mind to focus on the now. If your mind gives you unhelpful thoughts you can trigger your guard and clear your mind of gremlins. This gives you a little pattern of thinking: peace and calm, cluttering thoughts creeping in and then clearing them. It's a very useful little cycle or mind pattern. It is the nature of the mind to think, so rather than keep cleaning it up, why not start to build strong thought patterns that support you by replacing those negative thought patterns with newer, empowering thought patterns of your choice? As we journey through the jungle we don't always need to clear the way; we need a range of approaches to suit the terrain we are travelling through. So now we are talking about creating some basic positive thought patterns plus the ability to develop thinking patterns to enable your mind to support you whatever the terrain you are travelling through. Bright, sunny and dry or dark, tangled and heavy with moisture.

So the trick is, don't bother trying to stop thinking about something that is unhelpful; you'll just get more unwanted thoughts. Simply start making up your mind to replace the unwanted, unhelpful thoughts with something you want. Know how to work with the nature of your mind to look after and support yourself and make sure you get the best; just make sure your mind knows how to do that exactly as you know is best for you. Directing your thoughts for every stage and eventuality will enable you to thrive, not strive through your jungle journey.

Full steam ahead

So often the programmes we have learnt to run in our minds are part of our subconscious mindset, if you like. It doesn't matter WHO WE LEARNT these patterns from or WHY WE CHOSE to learn these patterns because we are dealing with our today, the here and now, and your ability to make today and your tomorrows work for you.

Some people spend years blaming someone else or some other time but for me this just makes us victims and still leaves us stuck! It blithely ignores the fact that we all have magnificent personal power which we can easily release today and in all of our tomorrows. When in crisis it's good to go to an expert who can help move us on, solve our problems and get us closer to what we want, but just don't forget we can do a lot for ourselves. Just as physically we look after our bodies and physical health, so we can easily look after our minds and keep them performing in tip-top condition so that, just like our bodies, they support us on our journey through the jungle of life.

Sometimes, we hit roadblocks in our mind and then finding a specialist to help us remove these blocks is a positive step so that we can enjoy today and flourish. To maximise this support and specialist help we can do a lot for ourselves and benefit from using our personal power, allowing our minds to work for us and not against us.

As I'm sure you've figured out by now, I work as a ChapWell

Method Coach one to one, and my work focuses on helping people remove barriers to their personal success and leaving their time with me with more tools than they started with as well as a way forward that works for them! Sometimes I come across something big that hinders my personal growth and development, and I no longer let it get in my way; I either clear it or seek specialist help so I can continue to grow and be the best I can be. In just the same way, if I have something hindering my physical wellbeing, I first try to sort it myself and if there's no improvement I seek specialist help. I just wonder why we are happy to work on our bodies but still shy away from working on our minds. More and more of my work is telling me it is because we just don't know how; yes, we know what we shouldn't be doing, but we don't know how to change those downer habits. I didn't know until my late thirties, and that's why I love it when young people come on my courses as well as all the other 'pretty normal bunch of people' from all walks of life.

Power boosting or chipping away?

I wonder how much of the negative thinking that you now order your guard to clear is self-criticism? Maybe even veiled self-criticism? By that I mean thinking critically of a loved one. When we criticise others we are frequently criticising ourselves; if a child then really we are saying 'If I was a better parent this wouldn't be happening'; if a partner then 'If I was a better partner/attracted a better partner I wouldn't have this problem', if a job 'Is this the best I can do?' and so on. Very often rather than boost ourselves to develop, we mentally beat ourselves up and others too, misguidedly thinking this will improve our performance. Added to that, what kind of relationships are we building, I wonder? I repeat, the only thing we have any control over is ourselves, and that's enough isn't it? (I am not at this point referring to our responsibility as parents/carers when we have a guiding, nurturing role until our children reach maturity.) Once we are grown and we have no need of being parented, who provides the love, care and nurturing through life's ups and downs? Do we look for someone else to do it and counterbalance the inner critic or do we do it for ourselves?

Be your best friend ever

If you make a mistake and get something wrong, do you reflect on what you would like to do next time and forget it? Or do you immediately criticise yourself, even call yourself unkind names? Would you treat your best friend like that? Imagine your best friend said they felt as if they were not doing at all well? What would you do, say or think? Cheer them on, cheer them up, help them overcome this hurdle or would you criticise them, agree they are useless, and need to get themselves together and all those other downer numbers? How do you treat yourself? How do you cheer yourself on through your days, hours and moments? If you are running late for an appointment what do you do? Mentally bash yourself up for not leaving earlier, blame someone else, think all sorts of unhelpful, maybe unkind thoughts about yourself and others? I think you are probably getting my meaning here. We can be our most reliable, loyal and available best friend, or our own worst enemy. What are you choosing to be? Do you know that no matter what happens you'll nurture and look after yourself and only feed your mind with motivating, nourishing thoughts to support you whatever comes your way?

What if you knew you are always safe?

What if you knew that no matter what happens in your life you will always be able to trust yourself to take you gently through the experience, based in peace and calm, so you can gather the learning and go on to better times? What if you knew you could easily create something better and more suited to what you want and need and all the while confidently travel through your jungle?

Trade negative for positive

When things are challenging, in good and bad times, I believe the most essential thing for us all is to feel safe. To be confident we will be able to support ourselves in all ways, knowing our intentions are good. At the very least we'll get some very valuable information that will help us grow, becoming stronger and wiser. We need to know our best friend will always be there, right beside us through this jungle journey of our life, so that we feel safe and able to push through the boundaries of our past experience and create ways to live that suit our NOW, our dreams and desires. Sure in the knowledge that we will fully approve, support and love ourselves. It's simple to do this, so why don't we? We have the choice: boosting or draining thoughts. The real problem here is that often we haven't learnt or been taught the magic: the simple fact that we can choose our thoughts. Rather than worrying, nagging, negative thoughts, you can pick thoughts to power the wonder of you, if you know how. It's always your choice: power up or nag down, you choose! We've all learnt to choose 'keeping safe' thoughts and someone else's thinking patterns that they learnt from someone else based on what they knew then, designed for someone else's jungle.

> A problem is only a lost item looking for its solution. Old, tried and tested solutions no longer fit or else there is no problem looking.
>
> ChapWellian saying circa 105

Important tip!

If you find yourself resisting this exercise you need it more than any other! I always find the exercises and situations where I start feeling resistance have the biggest wins. If you start to think of resistance as a signal to start learning, be alert. As you are just moving out of your comfort zone, resistance can become a useful indicator that you are changing and shifting things about. So consider resistance not as a signal to stop but just look and prepare yourself before you leap. Where's the harm here? Resistance is not keeping you safe, it's keeping you stuck right now! You want something to change, don't you? Maybe a little voice in your head or a familiar face is saying 'You don't believe that' or 'It's not that simple'. What you are thinking now is your choice: did you let an old programme of thought run or did you choose for you, for your now? I just wonder what you chose, the same or something better, more suited to your now?

Exercise – Turbo-Boosting Thoughts

Now pick and mix

Look down the list on the next page and just pick four or five that you feel drawn to. Do not try to justify or explain your choices; just accept, because it's likely your subconscious has guided you to what you need and that is a great starting place. This is a great exercise in trusting yourself and listening to your inner guidance! If you aren't sure which ones to choose, then pick the ones you feel most uncomfortable about and be brave! Why not? Your best friend – YOU – is there to cheer you on.

If you really cannot choose let the universe decide, be that luck or your spiritual beliefs; it is up to you. You can do this by writing out the positive thoughts, one thought per piece of paper. Put them in a bag and pick out five pieces of paper. A bit like a raffle but you win at every pick! You'll be amazed at how right for you your win turns out to be.

Start picking and enjoy!

We are all unique and have different needs but if you think of this as a 'brain diet' the list covers the essential things for your basic 'brain diet'. You can then select a diet that equips you to travel your jungle now. As your life unfolds you may wish to add in and take away things depending what is happening in your life. Just stick to five as a maximum number, otherwise you may find you'll forget!

Turbo- Boost Thoughts

I am gorgeous	I am helpful	I am enough
I am safe	I am happy	I am exactly how I need to be
I have everything I need to thrive	I am relaxed	I enjoy the best of everything
I am loved	I am clever	I deserve the best of everything
I am lovable	I am intelligent	I deserve good things
I have a great sense of humour	I am calm	I am secure
I am interesting	I am confident	I solve problems easily
I am worthwhile	I am motivated	It is easy for me to relax
I am strong enough	I trust in life	I trust myself
I easily prosper	I am healthy	I am good enough
Everything is OK	I am OK	I enjoy growing and learning
Mistakes help me grow, learn and choose	Any result is a great opportunity to choose	I am fearless

Everything is working out perfectly	It is what it is, I am safe	I am powerful
I am strong	I am flexible	My uniqueness adds to the world
There is plenty for everyone	I love and cherish myself	Everything is going along just fine
I am surrounded by peace and calm	I have and can create all I need	I thrive and flourish
I am so lucky	I attract all good things	I am blessed

The 'state' you're in

You may think that by sorting your thoughts you are missing vital parts of who you are but it works like this. No matter what you are doing and how you are feeling, calm or stressed, you are in a 'state'. Your state is made up of three things — actions, feelings and thoughts. Change any one of those and the others will follow. Feel happy and your body and thoughts will follow. Start slumping your body and hunching your shoulders and your thoughts and feelings follow. So by choosing your thoughts you are changing your state and by power boosting them, packing them with energy, you are accelerating them to become a part of you, giving you all the power and energy to create and attract what you want.

Create your own turbo-boosters

I hope I have made a big point of this method allowing the uniqueness of you to shine through. As time goes on or even as you start you'll want to create your own turbo-boosting thoughts as well as use the starter selection. Whatever you choose is absolutely fine so long as you follow the rules of turbo-boosting.

3 turbo- boost rules!

Your new thoughts must be stated in the

- **Positive** – Not a hint of negatives please.

- **Present time** – As if it exists now, is a fact, has happened, you have it or whatever it is you are turbo-boosting.

- **Your own words** – We all have words or a lexicon that we use in our everyday language and our mind recognises them. Better still our subconscious minds will believe them much more quickly; after all, it's how and what we usually think, say and respond.

Watch your language

This is a good time to introduce monitoring your language, both spoken and in thought. Start listening to yourself and how you express yourself in thought and out loud. If your turbo-boosts, thoughts or spoken words are stated as **wanting, trying, and needing you will only get more**

wanting, needing and trying! Who wants that? By opting for these words you are turbo-boosting them and giving them energy to exist. It works with the universal law of attraction based on the simple science that everything is made up of energy. Just think about it: if someone says something negative to you or even shouts, you pick up on that negative energy quickly. Just because you cannot see it doesn't mean it doesn't exist. Has anyone seen a good mood walking around lately or do you know what pure happiness, without its cause, looks like?

So when creating your turbo-boosters just make sure you check them against the three simple turbo-boost rules and all is done!

Some other language tips

Whilst you get used to being aware of your language start training yourself to give out positive energy rather than negative. It's not just your listener who's hearing the negative but it's you too. Every time you push out negative energy you experience a negative thought to go with it, just boosting your negative state. This puts a downer on your relationship with yourself and also with whomever you are communicating with. If you are communicating then you have a relationship, even if it is in passing, for example with a salesperson. It makes sense to make it work so you can feel good about the interaction and boost your wellbeing feelings as well. It never ceases to amaze me how people seem to think that negative communication can get what you want. It may in the very short term but it leaves you with a negative experience too – that's only fine if that's what you want to create.

Our language has a subconscious too

Or rather a subtext. Here's a few to get you started and start playing with in your everyday language to get the result you want.

Words that imply possibility, a reasonable option – can, may, possible, likely – these words are good to use in thought/ conversation with yourself and others to introduce new ideas and options. You can decide to practice the ChapWell Method or you can choose to not bother and get more of what led you to read this book. Or you can choose to skip this chapter and start with goal setting so you can get cracking on what you want to achieve. How do you prefer to make decisions: using ideas and options or directions? How do you respond to thoughts and words of necessity such as must, will, have to, should? How many times have you said to yourself: I must lose weight, I must go to the gym, and it hasn't stuck? Perhaps if you gave yourself an option talking-to it would work better?

I am a great options person and find them motivating. Currently I am freezing, sitting writing in the middle of a renovation project and putting on heating isn't an option and I'm fed up with it! So my current thoughts go like this, *'What do you want? Your old home or this beautiful house where you can grow your business, see your clients, run courses, lots of possibilities?'* Well for me it's a no brainer; I'm on my way and this time next year it will be a faint memory, even less than that. Then I feel myself getting excited and my mood instantly lifts. I also do a bit of visualisation or daydreaming to bring my future into my now.

The 3Ds – Directed Day Dreaming

Earlier I introduced you to the gem daydreaming as a form of self-hypnosis. Something most of us did naturally as children! Sadly, frequently we were trained to 'pack it in' and get real and pay attention by well-meaning adults. Well, I was, anyway! So, as we grow into young people and adults, somewhere along the way we leave behind an awesome self-development tool that most of us spent childhood perfecting. Lucky for us all, the knack of daydreaming comes back quickly, or maybe never leaves us. So with a bit of direction it is an easy way to support and release our personal power!

Start using the 3Ds

Start daydreaming your turbo-boosting thoughts too. Imagine yourself doing, being and acting with those things in place. Really allow your powerful imagination to let you experience your turbo-boosters in action. Your daydreams can be as bizarre as you choose; you're safe as they are daydreams and will always have a happy ending for you!
  Enjoy creating the you that accepts and loves yourself; get used to seeing, feeling and watching yourself turbo-boosted. Gradually the subconscious mind starts to accept it as true, which it is, and accelerates your power. You find yourself living it; wouldn't you choose to live that way rather than the critic's way? What would you prefer to have, a critic or a supporter on your shoulder, whispering in your ear? So next time you are waiting, perhaps sitting on a train, having a quick break, allow yourself a 3D moment. Some of you may do this already but instead you use this precious moment to worry and frighten yourself

with possibilities that haven't happened and are unlikely to happen, you hope! Pick one of your turbo-boosts and daydream what you will do, feel, be with your turbo-boost fully installed. Not only will this build you up, but it will also programme you to bring it into your world in whatever way you allow.

Look deep into your eyes

Many famous hypnotists have used this line and now you can use it too, on yourself. I do this every morning as I wash my face, clean my teeth and do anything else that's needed!!

Don't bother imagining that! Anyway to give your turbo-boosting statements a fast track to inner knowing, just look in the mirror, look deeply into your eyes, notice how beautiful they are and say aloud your turbo-boosters – I am … I have … and so on. Keep looking deeply into your eyes and repeating whilst you carry out your morning mirror work. Some people sing in the bathroom; you do your turbo-boosting now. Morning, noon and night, there's a lovely opportunity to boost yourself; now why wouldn't you do that?

And for when you have more time, about 10/15 minutes and/or before you allow yourself to drift off to sleep, visit your comfy chair and install those turbo-boosting thoughts deep into your subconscious.

Exercise - Comfy Chair Turbo- Boost

Remembering the safety instructions, make sure you are safe to 'go within' and remove your awareness from your surroundings. Take yourself into trance just by returning to your 'safe comfy chair place'. You can use these instructions if you need to as you take yourself into trance quickly and easily by returning to your 'comfy chair place'.

Key points of this exercise

- Go into deeper relaxation using your 'comfy chair'.

- Daydream your way into feeling, being, doing, speaking and thinking with your turbo-boosts installed, one by one.

- Allow your imagination to really explore how you feel and think and what you do with all your boosts installed.

- Return to your 'comfy chair' and allow yourself to drift into sleep or bring yourself back into the now.

- Carry on with your day only when you are fully alert.

1. Get yourself comfortable and in a safe place where you can go inwards without being disturbed for about 10 to 15 minutes.

2. **Power Breaths** – Take 3 deep breaths, breathe in to the count of 3, pause and release your breath to the count of 3. Then allow your breathing to settle to normal.

3. Imagine going down your 10 step staircase, through the door into your safe place.

4. Enjoy being in your special, safe place; notice the colours, sounds, smells, the way things are placed, notice shapes and form.

5. When you are ready sink into your 'comfy chair'.

6. Whilst in your comfy chair begin to allow your mind to daydream yourself having, being, feeling, doing, enjoying all of your turbo-boost thoughts.

7. Spend time making sure your turbo-boost daydreams are colourful and bright; imagine your feelings building and feel your power as you enjoy the feelings your turbo-boosts give you. Notice how your body feels and moves with your turbo-boosts installed.

8. As you work your way through each turbo-boost statement, make sure you can easily recognise

9. each one and have a clear picture of you enjoying each turbo-boost separately and together. See yourself moving, speaking, interacting with your turbo-boost thoughts as a natural part of you.

10. When you are sure you know what your turbo-boost thoughts look, sound or feel like, just relax and enjoy the peace and calm of your safe place. Relax into your comfy chair if you are going into a deep sleep now.

11. If you are getting on with your day, when you are ready leave your 'Comfy Chair', go through the door and take your 10 step staircase back up into the now.

12. Stretch, blink and make sure you are fully alert before you carry on with your day. **Remember** you need to wake yourself up, just as if you had been in a deep sleep, before carrying on with the rest of your day.

Scribble your way to power

It is important to write out your turbo-boosters; it's a really good way to get them firmly entrenched in your long-term memory and subconscious states of being or power tools! I have a little notebook by my bed in which I put down all the brilliant and wild ideas that come to me during the night. I also put my turbo-boosters in this little booklet and spend a few moments each day, either first thing in the morning or last thing at night, writing out my current turbo-boosting statements, those ones that I am working on installing right now. I really scribe them, write them with a flourish, complete with doodles and flowers! Great for setting me up to visit my 'comfy chair' and slip into a peaceful, restorative sleep. Now why wouldn't you end your day like that, I wonder?

Maybe you prefer to type them into your tablet; that's good too. Just spend time making them as beautiful, stunning, eye catching, or whatever does it for you as possible. I like beautiful things; you may prefer strong – just make sure you realise your way is the best so long as it is positively powerful. No dark sides please. If they creep in rub them out, change them, do what you want to get rid of them. They don't belong to your life any more.

Doodle your power

Whenever I get a chance, maybe I am watching a TV programme or chatting on the phone, I make a point of doodling my turbo-boosts. Sometimes I don't even write the words, I just allow my mind to draw what they would look like if they were a thing! Sometimes I get simple flowers, other times I am obviously much more creative and have very grandiose doodles; whatever, it is a fun, simple way to do your turbo-boosts. You'll probably come up with some ideas yourself: whatever gets you focused, enjoying and boosting your power works.

Inner critic or best friend?

I remember once being very confused about following, hearing or feeling my inner voice, my inner wisdom. I was starting to learn about the ego and how it can be a good servant when using it as 'me' without any links or attachments. However it can also become an exhausting master if allowed to run the show and insist on links such as I am (is that good enough?), I have (is that enough?) and so on.

Research and some very clever people show us that we have ourselves (our true selves) and we have the ego that is never satisfied and wants more and more, driving us on to strive after more, usually material or things external to us. I'm all for material things: comfort and enough to live a life that is not a constant struggle to make things work for me. The ego, though, tends to unbalance us, if allowed to run the show, disrupting and ignoring a need for balance between inner and outer needs. I then found myself unsure how I would know if my inner voice was my inner voice or my inner critic, fear-based thinking or ego. Then I realised it was simple: my inner voice, guidance, wisdom, gut, whatever you like to call it, would always be positive, never critical. It may tell me not yet, or wait, but will always say there is something even better coming up for me, or find out more and so on! Always supportive, always helping me grow and develop and never putting me on the back foot. Brilliant! Always looking for the possibilities, alerting me to choice and to reflect on my previous experience, not to beat myself but to equip myself to go forward and fulfil my potential. So that's what the next chapter is all about, accessing your inner wisdom, your brilliance, no strings, no 'If I hads', no 'If I was'; it's all there for us if only we knew how to listen.

Chapter 5
The Wisdom in YOU

Key 4 – Your inner wisdom

Have you ever

- found yourself stuck, not sure which way to go?

- worried about what is the right thing to do?

- searched for solutions and ended up just chasing around and around in your head?

- made a decision and regretted it almost immediately?

- missed opportunities because you just didn't recognise them, or worse, feared them?

This fear-based thinking takes up a lot of energy and rather than power ourselves up, wears us down and out. Key 4 allows you to still think things through but enables you to do just that rather than boost your fears, uncertainties and feelings of insecurity. To solve a problem, to make a decision and to create the life that you want, big or small, you need to gather all your information, the facts, the potential and your resources and decide what is the best course of action for you. As I remind you again, the only person you have any control over is you! How you access the 'you' when you are under pressure is the thing and Key 4 allows you to do just that.

Who lives in a bubble?

I have read many personal development books that have assured me I could have anything I want; all I have to do is go for it. I believe that to be absolutely true but what it doesn't seem to take into account is that there is a very large group of us that have responsibilities to people we love, regardless of whether we like them! I needed the 'Get what you want in your life' version that recognised I lived in a real world and didn't live in a bubble. Yes, I could follow their advice and guidance and get what I want, but at what cost to everything else that was important to me? We are complex individuals and different things are important to us but it's rare to meet an individual who can thrive on only one thing or one goal being important. Take me for example my 'important to me' list, which goes something like this and in no priority order: family, friends, work, helping, fun, exercise, money, home, travel, learning, knowledge. Not one of those things would enable me to feel happy and content if I focused on it, or had only one thing in my life. So it makes sense to me to equip ourselves to form a balanced life with the ability and option to shift those balances to meet our needs as we grow and develop and travel through the jungle of life.

Regardless of should and ought tos

We all have a lot of should and ought tos in our lives which can crowd us. You should do this, you must do that, now this and then that and on and on. So it makes sense to look after the key ingredient in your life, you of course! To regularly make time for yourself and check in that what you are creating is right for you and critically is the best balance for you.

Keep up to date with who you are

So I decided my first focus, to weave through my busy life, was to really get to know me at this time in my life! I realised I had limited control over what happens but I have full control over my choices and how to react towards and experience this time in my life. I also realised we change and develop and this remains as true now as it was then. As time goes on and I work with more people this realisation has been proved true time and time again. In fact it is a key component of the coaching paradigm.

Put simply, a lot of our struggle and problems come from applying old patterns of thinking, problem solving and approaches to new situations in our life. It is very naive to think we don't develop, grow and change, but for some reason we don't seem to naturally learn how to develop our thinking in line with our needs rather our and others' experience. So for me, my clients and my delegates, I developed these easy ways to keep in touch with your current you and your current needs to be able to check what a balanced life is for you NOW. I tend to use them when I feel guided to, need more information to make a decision, or am feeling I am struggling. You choose what will trigger you to check out your needs and balance. For my clients and course delegates it's where we start. Do you know what your balance is and what it contains?

Check in as your lifelong coach

It makes sense that you should learn how to be your best coach, your biggest supporter, fan and helper towards your success in life and those things that are important to you. Only you will know, truly know, YOU. So it makes sense YOU are your first line coach. No appointments necessary, no long journeys, no time wasted waiting for your coach. Coaching and its benefits, at a time to suit you and your unique needs, is only a thought away for you now.

Getting in touch with you

Start listening to yourself, your true self, not your programming, not your shoulds, woulds and coulds but your absolute needs and wants to be you. Ekhart Tolle's book *A New Earth* starts to lead us back from our ego to our real self where, I believe, true happiness lies for each of us. Scary, isn't it? I am not suggesting you give up all material things, or throw up your job or radically change your life, just that you start to listen to yourself and allow your inner spirit or soul (whatever you want to call it) to guide you, support you and throw out the ego critic who just wants more, more and even more. By the ego critic I mean any descriptors of who you are that associate you with external things to measure your worth. For example I am a mother, I am a teacher, I am a coach and so on. These things now become opportunities for you to reveal your true self, not a vehicle for your ego to insist you should be better, be more, have more and everything else the ego demands.

Just you

Stop for a moment and think of who you are. Not who you are to others but who you are without any links to anything external to you. Wouldn't you like to be sure you really know who you are? Stripped of all the labels, successes, failures, others' perceptions, friends, family, can you get to love and like who you are? Are you sure of your answer? Does your answer trip off your tongue? Do you accept and love all parts of you including those bits that you don't feel so proud of for whatever reason?

Sort out your roles

If we consider the roles in our lives as opportunities to express who we are and our purpose in life then that starts to put another spin on things. So list all of the wonderful roles you inhabit in your life – daughter, son, brother, sister, carer, girl/boyfriend, partner, teacher, job role etc. Make your list as full as possible, but try not to spend lots of time on it; just jot down the roles that come into your mind over the next few minutes. It's OK to add to the list later if you like. Forget the ego critic who may say that it's a lot or it's too much, just make the list below.

My roles

Now put at the top of the list, in big letters, ME. Yes, it's OK to make ME more important than all those other roles as the ME of you brings that unique touch to your roles that makes you special; you are the brother, sister, lover, partner, essential to that role. So let's start enjoying the YOU or ME and draw strength from yourself, get to know yourself, love yourself and understand what made you create and attract those roles in your life.

Exercise – 'Must Have' Pyramid

What is Important to YOU?

This exercise helps you find out the Must Haves in your life to help you know and recognise the **authentic** you.

Get together ten pieces of paper, big enough to write one word on each. I find post-its work brilliantly for this exercise as it stops the ten pieces of paper getting lost or muddled!

1. Clear your mind using **Power Breaths.**

2. Now ask yourself, 'What's important to me?' **Only accept one-word answers**. One-word answers are important. As soon as you start putting your answers into sentences you'll start justifying and explaining, and the conscious mind will start changing things. Allow the first thing that comes into your mind to be your answer. Accept it and

write it down. Avoid justifying your answers; if you get the same answer just say thanks and ask the question again.

3. Write down your one-word answers on your post-its or pieces of paper. One word per piece of paper until you have a word on each of your 10 pieces of paper.

4. If you have a repeat answer, that's fine, just ask yourself the question again, 'What's important to me?' until you get something new. If you get stuck, use **Power Breaths** to help you to focus! (Remember this is a valuable little tool you now have instantly at your disposal.)

5. Now arrange your pieces of paper into a pyramid, putting the most important at the top and the least important at the bottom of your pyramid. Using post-its helps as you can stick them to a large sheet of paper for you to look at.

The important thing is to go for one-word answers, with no sentences and no judgements on what comes up! My pyramid, showing the most important at the top, looks like this:

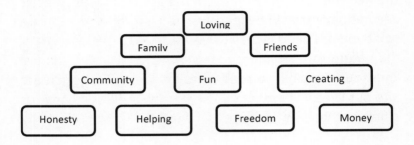

Most important versus least important

Ranking your 'must haves' is a vital part of this process. Ranking allows you to identify your most important in terms of percentage or how important it is to you. For a balanced life you need all aspects to show up, so for me I like to do things with love, or for the love of my fellow people. Ranking is not about doing without, but it allows you to see all of the things that are essential to your wellbeing, the uniqueness of you. For example money ranks last for me but it is still important, critical really, as it frees me to focus on all the other things. So don't forget any one of your 'must haves'; just start to be aware how they each contribute to your wellbeing and a balanced life for you. I had a client who said she loved her job, and she didn't mind working long hours as she enjoyed her job. However, she was starting to feel her job was taking over her life and there was no time for anything else, none of the other essential things for her. Rather than blame her job, she was able to work out what she needed and look for similar work that allowed her enough time to meet all her needs. In fact, she discussed the problem with her boss and got her hours changed; the money was less but it mattered more that she had time for one of her other passions, painting, as in decorating houses! I believe half of the problem of getting what you or I need is really knowing what we need and, in the nature of humankind, it is rarely one thing! Once we know our complex mix then we can work at ways to bring it into our lives. I urge you to be open to experiment and try different things to find what suits you best.

Essential elements for you

You now have a good idea of what is important for you at this time in your life. As you grow, develop and reach different phases of your life, your 'essential elements' MAY change and become clearer – that's fine and worth remembering. I like to do a check as part of setting my intentions (Key 5) for the New Year and see what's right for me now, not last year but now! I never set New Year's Resolutions but just consider and decide on my intentions for the year, check them against my 'must haves' and then enjoy the journey. That way I am always clear about my direction and able to change and adapt as the year unfolds, even take up any unplanned opportunities life brings if they suit me. No broken resolutions for me, just my intentions and those steps I take to create them.

Exercise: Back to the Now – 3 Parts

- How your roles can help you express your 'must haves'

- How your other activities help you enjoy and create the 'must haves'

- How you treat yourself to your 'must haves'

Presuming you are doing this for the first time, the next exercise helps you check if you are fully expressing the stuff that is important to you in your life. Do both exercises to help you find where you are able to express those things that are essential to your being. In short, it may be a recognised role, for example mother, son, daughter, which provides an opportunity to express those important things that make up the uniqueness of you. If you recognise what you need you can easily create ways to meet that need and live a fuller, more satisfied life.

Review your pyramid and ask yourself, 'How am I bringing these things into my life?'

Here's me expressing myself in the roles I have in my life at the moment:

My roles	My essential being I am able to express in this role
Mother	Loving, caring, helping, friend, family, fun, community, honesty, freedom
Freelance Trainer/Coach	Loving, friend, fun, honesty, helping, freedom, money, family, communication
Friend	Loving, caring, fun, honesty, helping, freedom, community, extended 'family'

Now your turn

Put all of your roles in the list and enjoy finding out how they give you an opportunity to express your essential being, those things important for you to have and be in your life. Let your list be a unique expression of yourself.

My roles	My essential being I am able to express in this role

Nourish your essentials

Are there any gaps? Are there things missing? Is the balance right for you? How can you easily balance things out? More of this and less of that? A lot of research and investigation has been done on how important it is for us to live in a way that meets our authentic self. How we need to be true to ourselves, to be truly content and happy. How the absence of meeting our essential needs can lead to a general feeling of dissatisfaction through to stress, anxiety and even depression. In this modern world we sometimes turn to props to fill the gap such as smoking, overeating and worse, all these things that will in time chip away at our wellbeing and inevitably our physical health. I am not going to repeat those theories here. I mention them now to help you understand how powerful this exercise is for you by allowing you to steer your life to meet your needs, balanced to suit the uniqueness of you.

I have worked with many people who frequently decide work is their problem, then set about looking for reasons to support this, choosing to focus all the blame on work, not realising they are just giving their power away. We all have the power to create balance in our lives; often we just haven't learnt how to do that. The first step is knowing what YOU need to balance and this exercise helps you understand you, your needs and balance. Work is a part of our lives but not the whole; it is a part that needs balancing and this can easily be done when you know your essential needs. Incidentally, by work I mean those things you need to do, from cleaning the toilet, to running a household, to caring for a sick relative to paid employment. Even the most tedious task can be an opportunity for balance and rest using the tools in this book. I switch my mind to my virtual comfy chair as I clean the toilets – well, I ask you, who wouldn't?

Audit Your Essentials Exercise

This exercise is useful to check, at a glance, if the balance is aligned with your pyramid. Include all your activities. Here's an example:

My must-haves	How I can express this more in my life
Helping/caring	My work, training, coaching, writing, volunteer work, my family, friends
Freedom	Long distance walks, travelling, holidays, free time

Now insert your 'must haves' and consider the balance. Ask yourself if it seems OK for you and how it matches your pyramid. You are the judge; you will know if you need to shrink something down to result in a more balanced life for you. For example, if you consider the above example, there is a lot of caring and helping in this life. First look at the freedom 'must have' which has fewer opportunities for expression: is that OK with your pyramid? Is freedom less important than helping and caring? Or is it the same? Start looking at your role chart to see if there is a balance of expression as to how things need to be for you now. Is the balance right for you? Does it align with your pyramid? Your life, your judgement, your choice, but could you make it more balanced by reducing one role's demands and increasing another? Maybe, maybe not.

I urge my clients and delegates to be playful with this and not opt for any massive changes. Rather, gently alter things and be aware of the changes; see how you feel, what you think of the change, how things go and then maybe make another change to find out if it suits the uniqueness of who you are.

In time it becomes a more normal practice to plan our time, making decisions based on our needs, and you should allow yourself time to develop the habit. Remember there is no right or wrong, just your jungle journey, moving forward and not stuck in the mire!

My must-haves	How I can express this more in my life

Daily practice

The real payback with this is to make it a daily practice to carry out an audit just to review your day and how it met your needs. A notebook helps us keep track and if you haven't already started keeping a notebook of your jungle journey, maybe now's a good time to start. Who needs to keep all this in their head anyway! Keep a record of your pyramid and then at the end of each day list against your 'must haves' how you have met them today. If there is any imbalance you can make a mental note to bring it into your next day or write a turbo-booster to constantly remind yourself and attract more 'xxxxx' into your day. Reflecting on your pyramid each day, how you have met the balance on a daily basis, is a good way to start to get to know yourself, and work out where you forget your needs and allow life and others to take more than you have to give. Please note that you always allow it; only you have the power to change the balance and the balance that you have now is one you have created. So why not create a balance that suits you better still?

Remember peace and calm

Just a reminder that these are the things that are important and essential to you. My list does not contain peace and calm but yours may and that is fine. I just view peace and calm as our natural state in which we enjoy being who we are. It just means that as well as using the ChapWell tools to encourage a normal setting of peace and calm in your mind and body, you need to bring into your life activities that enable you to experience more peace and calm such as meditation, yoga, fishing, whatever is peace and calm for you. When I was grieving the loss of my husband I needed very high levels of solitude and rest which showed up in my 'must haves' exercise; for me it was walking, gardening, reiki and reading. I also used my comfy chair and other tools to help me stay peaceful and calm during this period of change in my life.

I truly believe that, no matter what your personal situation is, you can work in opportunities to meet your needs as well as meeting all of your responsibilities. That's why an important part of my method is about weaving the techniques into your everyday life. This creates the confidence and security that you can feel within yourself: through good and bad times, you know you are able to thrive, learn and grow, not just survive.

If you find you have the same answers for any of your 'must haves', move them into a box together and see if anything else comes to mind. You get the picture: make your own list, listen to your inner voice and think about all the things you do and say, and the people you mix with.

It's an easy way to get to the root of uneasiness and do something positive about it. If one or more of your 'must haves' are not being met then it's very easy to spot using this exercise. You can then set about creating a better balance for you.

Experiment with wellbeing

It doesn't have to be a big change; it can just be something small. For example if you find you don't have enough fun in your life do something to bring in fun: watch a funny show on TV, go to the mirror and pull a funny face, start making room for fun every day. Set a goal to bring in the fun to enable you to live the way you need to live. Start small and see how it feels, then gently grow it. Treat your wellbeing like an important experiment – if you don't like what you have, get, feel or see, just tweak it and see what changes follow. Start to feel the power to create your jungle.

Your true purpose in life

I have noticed over the past couple of years an increase in the desire and need of people (myself included) to find out their true purpose in life. Would you like to know what your true purpose in life is? I spent years wondering what it was, and asked people who knew me well but never accepted any answers because my ego decided they just weren't big enough, glam enough, smart enough. I went on courses and read more books than you could shake a stick at to try and find out that elusive life purpose. I spent four mind-blowingly boring days finding out what my values and beliefs were, only to see in front of me what I already knew, give or take a couple of words.

Guess what? You already know

Relaxing my conscious mind through self-hypnosis, I learnt how to ask myself and actually listen to the answer; listen to myself. All was clear and added to that I had actually talked about what I truly wanted to do since I was in my late twenties! All my steps, studies and everything I had done and that had happened in my life was always leading me towards my life purpose. So for all those wishing to know their life purpose out there, you already know, you just need to learn to listen unconditionally!

Exercise: Tapping into Your Wisdom

This exercise helps you to start to listen and trust yourself by listening to your inner wisdom, guidance, whatever you want to call it. Each of us has an incredible amount of wisdom that we rarely tap into to ask specific questions. Too often we just react to the information buried deep in our subconscious, rather than consider it, reflect on it, wonder if it is true for us now, and use it to create new knowledge. On my courses I call it listening and talking to your intuition, your natural inner guidance and biggest supporter or fan.

Find somewhere where you can be undisturbed for at least 20–25 minutes, longer if you want for your first trip to your inner wisdom. Switch off phones and anything else that may interrupt you. If you struggle during the day to make a space for this, that's fine, do it before you go to sleep at night. Even if you fall asleep work will continue in your subconscious but after time, I hope you enjoy going there when you can come back and actively remember the learnings. The key thing is start to trust yourself and realise we are all born whole and meant to be our biggest cheerleaders.

Exercise Key Points

- relaxing both your mind and body

- going to your safe place

- going through a gate

- walking in the countryside

- following a winding path

- meeting up with your older self (10 years older)

- having a conversation with yourself, asking questions, listening to the answers

1. **Power Breaths** – Start with your 3 deep breaths, count in your mind on your inward breath, 1, 2, 3 pause, and then count on your outward breath, 3, 2, 1 pause.

2. **Clear your mind** – Use your clear the mind techniques. Clear your mind, if thoughts wander in just let them wander out, put legs on them and watch them walk away. Or maybe you want to start counting the thoughts or maybe you choose to pick up a broom and sweep those thoughts right out of your head. Just choose the best way for you to clear your mind.

3. Imagine going down your stairs to your safe place; open the door and for a moment enjoy looking around your safe place.

4. Now sink into your 'comfy chair'. Feel that wonderful feeling of relaxation, peace and calm flow through your body and mind.

5. As you clear your mind and experience the wonderful feeling of relaxation, peace and calm, imagine you are going for a wonderful walk in the countryside. Imagine getting up from your comfy chair, leaving your safe place and going to another safe place in the countryside.

6. Feel the warmth of the sun, hear the sounds of the countryside around you and smell the smells in the beautiful clear air.

7. Now imagine there is a gate in front of you and you open the gate to walk along a winding path, all the time knowing you are perfectly safe. On either side of the path are fields and you enjoy looking around you, as far as your eyes can see, as you walk the path. This walk is your walk; enjoy the countryside around you: maybe there are wide open spaces, maybe woods. Enjoy the colours, the sounds and the smells. Feel the earth below your feet and take deep breaths of the clear pure air.

8. Notice the sky, maybe it's blue with white fluffy clouds drifting slowly along. Notice the warmth of the sun on you as you walk, totally safe, along the path. You can hear the sounds of the countryside

9. around you and you are totally at peace as you walk along, at your own pace, enjoying the beautiful countryside around you.

10. As you walk along you continue to notice all the beautiful growth of nature, noticing the colours all around you of the trees, the grass, any flowers you might see, the hedges or bushes; this is your peaceful walk and you will know what you see. Just notice the beauty all around you as you walk, perfectly safe, perfectly relaxed.

11. As you walk along your path you notice someone coming along the path towards you. Notice how they are walking slowly, as relaxed as you and enjoying their walk away from it all, totally relaxed. As they come closer you realise you recognise them: it's you, an older you, 10 years older. They are smiling and you say hello, they turn and you decide to walk with them.

12. The older you leads you to a small cluster of trees and you both walk through an opening. You can hear water gently flowing in a river and together you walk down to the edge of the river. By the river there is a clear, soft patch of grass surrounded by smooth rocks.

13. You both sit down, facing each other, leaning against the smooth rocks.

14. The older you asks you how you are and you begin to tell them.

15. Whilst you listen to their reply you notice how relaxed and happy the older you is.

16. You start to talk and listen to what the older you has to say, ask anything you want, and listen carefully to what they say... Perhaps you wish to ask them if you have all of your 'must haves' for now.

17. Or maybe you want to ask what your life purpose is? Listen carefully to the answer.

18. Stay as long as you want talking and listening to your older self. Relax and enjoy the conversation... ask all the questions, share all the thoughts you want; this is your time, so relax and just let things happen, accept what you hear, and ask whatever you want.

19. When you are ready to leave, give your older self a hug and thank them for their time, then slowly make your way back through the trees to the path.

20. Walk along the path reflecting on your time with your older self, enjoy the peaceful countryside all around you and relax.

21. When you are ready you see the gate up ahead and, bringing your memories of relaxation with you and your time with your older self, come back into the room, into the now.

22. Slowly stretch and open your eyes. Give yourself plenty of time to become fully alert, remember what day it is and gently think what next your day holds for you.

23. When you feel fully awake and alert you can now get on with the rest of your day.

Remember to allow yourself to become fully awake before carrying on with your day, exactly as you would after waking from a deep sleep.

Reflect on what you heard and what you felt prompted to ask!

The beauty of this exercise is it gives you information about you, what is buried in your subconscious mind, your inner wisdom and guidance. You may choose to act on the information you gather or you may choose to check out if the guidance works for you. I frequently do this exercise to help with big decisions or just for reassurance that everything is OK in the end. I love that wonderful saying that I heard for the first time in the film *The Best Exotic Marigold Hotel* which goes something like this: 'All will be well in the end and if it's not all well yet, then it's not the end!'

I love this exercise and find myself doing it frequently just to be reassured all is well and will be well. Whilst writing this book I have visited many times to ask if I am doing the right thing, taking time out from paid work to write this book. The answer has led me to understand that nothing is guaranteed but it's OK as this book is something I was meant to write; it is part of my life purpose. Now I am in a place where I have fully released any expectations and am just enjoying the process of writing, creating, bringing into reality a long-held dream!

So there are no magic answers but the truth, your truth.

A few quick tips

Sometimes people report they couldn't really see themselves, but just saw a shadow or felt the presence of another and that's fine. Your experience will be unique and absolutely what you need.

On another course a participant reported that instead of her meeting her older self she met herself as a child. I suggested next time, if her younger self joins her, just ask her why she is there. Knowing this participant I also suggested that maybe she had been so busy lately she hadn't been looking after her inner child; had she been 'playing' lately? When was the last time she did something just for fun? We all know we need both work and play and research has shown us we need to look after our 'inner child' as well as our grown up! After all, we can all feel unsafe, lost, confused, in need of guidance, bored, a lack of fun, can't we? Now start considering these feelings as indicators to change, grow and improve our wellbeing.

No perfects too

There are no perfects or absolutes in this exercise; you create your own hypnotic experience and in time you will trust yourself to give you exactly what you need. If you don't understand an answer then just ask your older self to explain!

Planning, reflecting and thinking

Remember – there is a time for action in our lives and also a time to restore, recharge, learn, and reflect. Think of all of these happening within a feeling of contentment, calm and peace. Begin to value those times as much as you value the doing times. You know the well-said saying, 'We are human beings not human doings', so enjoy being as much as you feel inclined to do.

If you are more of a doer don't panic

The funny thing is the more you build in relaxation and allow your mind to guide you the more you seem to get done and achieve. I know this seems a contradiction but it is true for me; my clients and those who have attended my courses all report this strange phenomenon. One day I will do some research and find out if it is more to do with the fact that you are living in the now, your confidence builds and you 'Don't sweat the small stuff' as Richard Carlson so brilliantly explains in his book. So many people who have found their way through meditation, yoga or all the other supportive practices tend to report the same in my experience.

Trust and understanding

Sometimes the answers I get back don't seem right to me and I realise I have found something that doesn't work for me here and now. I mentioned the workaholic earlier; that was me, so I'll give you another example of reflecting and thinking about what my subconscious thought or, if you like, my older self.

When I first started to realise that I was running back into my old ways of dealing with problems i.e. working harder and longer, I decided this had to stop. The message I got from my older self was that everything would be OK, but do you want the easy way or the hard way? I understood what this meant for me, yes, I would get through this time but did I want to do it through hard slog or acceptance and joy? I chose acceptance and joy!

I was very, very tired after caring for my husband during his illness and knew a break by resigning from my job was the only way out for me. I couldn't just draw back and reduce my input; I was too hardwired to make sure I gained approval at work for myself and from others. Remember I had to prove I was useful, I was good at what I did and I was good enough! So I decided to take the plunge after consulting my finances and realising a break of 6 months or even a year was manageable financially.

I didn't know how long I'd need but I also knew I couldn't go back. I needed to go forward, so I resigned from my well-paid position. I then began the long, slow process of building myself back up and using everything I knew, including continuing to learn and study. I say slow as I would rather it had been fast, my way. I mentioned the finances being OK but the scary bit was what if no one wanted to employ me after this? I knew this was just my ego playing tricks but still the fear felt real. What if no one knew me and my capacity to earn a good living had gone with it? Being someone that likes to plan ahead I realised I didn't know the answers and just had to trust in myself and my future. I took the time off; after a few months I was bored but still very tired so did a few little jobs along the way, but nothing that was permanent or long term. I did short jobs and worked, in fact, on average 2 to 3 days a week over a two-year period. So my plan changed and it worked. Now I wake up every morning excited about the day, eager to get started, flexible to carry out the tasks and enjoy a career that, for years, people have been telling me that I am good at!

All this came from listening to myself and then taking practical steps towards I knew not what, but it has never let me down, not once! I emphasise practical steps; work within your real boundaries, not imagined ones! If you are feeling worn down and cannot afford to give yourself a break from your job find a way you can give yourself some meaningful rest. Try the following exercise.

The Me Challenge: Learn to Treat Yourself

I ask many of my clients to try this approach especially when they feel time is at a premium in their lives. It just involves giving yourself a treat every day and keeping a record of your treats. The rule is that the treat can be anything you decide, so long as it costs you no more than nothing and it must be a different treat every single day.

It's a great habit to get into. Ask yourself, how can I treat myself today? Then spend time thinking of a treat for yourself and then treating yourself, not tomorrow but today. One client of mine who took **The Me Challenge** had treats ranging from a hot bubble bath surrounded by candles to 15 minutes with her phone switched off, sat in the park, just watching nature. She got as much fun planning and looking forward to her treats as she did enjoying them. She was also developing an important habit of thinking of herself, listening to her own needs and meeting them.

Try it and notice how you feel after a week of treating yourself. It really is a great booster and something to keep in your life forever! The Me Challenge is a great one to do with a partner, friend or relative too. At the end of the day or next time you meet sharing your treat records and experiences can be fun and doubles your bank of ideas.

Just to be clear, I'm not against treating yourself with something that costs if you can afford it. The important purpose of this exercise is to realise that you have everything you need to make yourself feel good, something that I believe we are beginning to overlook in this modern world we live in. This exercise helps you to find within you a never-ending supply of treats to support yourself and boost your wellbeing.

Clearing out tensions from the body too

More and more research is coming up with the evidence that demonstrates the link between our physical body and mental state. So it makes sense to clear your body of the results of negative thought patterns and what we frequently call stress. Since I have been doing this self-hypnosis exercise I have suffered far fewer migraines, one a year rather than one a month. Then when I think back and get caught with a migraine I realise I have not been regularly relaxing and clearing every part of my body. Clients have also reported improvements; as yet I haven't carried out any clinical research but we all know that relaxing every part of your body and mind is tremendously beneficial!

Exercise: Colour Your Mind and Body

Remember the bit about our state: that we work in a triad of thoughts, emotions and actions. If you change one thing the rest will follow, so this exercise changes the level of tension in your body allowing the mind and emotions to follow.

Get yourself comfortable, either sitting or lying. Try and make sure your back is straight and your legs and arms uncrossed. This will make sure you don't 'come to' with pins and needles or a stiff back from an awkward position.

Switch off phones and make sure you are in a safe place to go within and ignore the rest of the world. This exercise can take as long as you like but as a guide allow yourself about 15 minutes at least. Again as in all of the self-hypnosis exercises you can do this before you go off to sleep.

Key Points

- relaxing both your mind and body

- clearing the mind

- focus on each part of your body and imagine it is a colour

- clear the colour and boost it

- work all the way through the body

1. **Power Breaths** – Breathe in counting 1, 2, 3, pause and out 3, 2, 1, pause. Repeat for 8-12 breaths.

2. Allow your breathing to relax into a normal pace and then gently close your eyes.

3. Imagine that each part of your body has a colour. Allow each colour to come to you naturally and easily as you work your way from your head to your feet. The colour doesn't matter and repeat colours are allowed!

4. This is what you do. Look in your mind or, if you prefer, at your closed eyelids. Focus on clearing all the tension in your mind and then head by looking at the colour you see on your eyelids. Clear the colour so it is even, in tone, depth and clarity. Then inject brightness into the colour you see.

Whatever colour you see is just fine; this is your personal relaxation session. Just focus on clearing the colour so it is a clear, true colour, with no smudges, no shading, just a clear colour. Watch the colour clear for you. How you clear the colour is up to; let your imagination guide you. When the colour is clear and even in tone to suit you, gently move your focus on.

5. Now focus your mind on your neck. Again look at the colour before your closed eyes. Focus on clearing all the tension in your neck. Look at the colour you see on your eyelids or in your mind's eye and clear that colour so it is even, in tone, depth and brightness of colour. Continue to focus on clearing the colour until it is a clear colour with no smudges, no shading, just a clear colour. Watch the colour clear for you. Inject brightness into the colour so the colour is strong and even in tone. When it is clear and you are ready gently move your focus on.

6. Now focus on your shoulders. Again, look at the colour before your closed eyes. Focus on clearing all the tension in your shoulders by looking at the colour you see on your eyelids or imagining your shoulders as a colour. Continue clearing that colour so it is even, in tone, depth and brightness of colour. Clear this colour the same way you have for your head/mind and neck.

7. Continue travelling to each part of your body, allowing the colour to come to you and working on clearing the colour. Finally inject the colour with brightness and vibrancy. When you are happy the colour is strong, clear and vibrant then move onto the next body part – back, chest, arms, hands, tummy, hips, thighs, knees, lower legs, ankles and feet.

8. Once you have cleared your whole body, enjoy the wonderful relaxed feeling you have created and just allow your body to feel as if it is so light you could float.

9. If any colours come into mind and need clearing just gently clear them so you only enjoy pure colours before your eyes or in your imagination. These colours may be new colours or may be colours you had already cleared but now require deeper clearing. Feel yourself relaxing deeper into the chair, bed or floor as you do this.

10. Now just enjoy this time of total physical and mental relaxation and recharge.

11. You can stay in this state for as long as you want. When you are ready count yourself back from 1 to 10.

12. Open your eyes, stretch; give yourself enough time to come back into the now, the same as if you had been deeply asleep.

If time is short

I learnt this from a client who, like many of us, carried his tension in his neck. He combined Power Breaths and just focusing on clearing the colour in his neck throughout the day. It only takes 2/3 minutes but helps stop that build-up of tension, and in his case stopped the tension headaches he was constantly suffering from.

Allow yourself to develop in your unique way

Clients who have tried this on my courses have reported many different ways of creating and clearing their colours. One client reported painting the colour on or over the first colour they saw and being surprised what colour their paintbrush gave them. They then continued painting until the colour was just right for them.

Another client actually used a hose which first prepared/ cleaned the area for painting and then when ready automatically sprayed the colour on. So do not be surprised if you find your own way of 'relaxing your colours' and corresponding parts of the body. Relax and enjoy! Trust you mind to find its own way to relax and soothe you.

Remember no perfects please!

The Tale of the Wellian Horses

In ChapWell Land for a very long time the Wellians were the main carriers and traders bringing everything the ChapWellians needed from the north to their southern lands. The Wellians were renowned horsemen and were the only ones who could manage the horses, loaded with wares, walking along the perilously narrow mountain passes. Other merchants had tried but failed to successfully navigate and lead their horses through the treacherous mountain passes and the dark, dangerous jungles.

In spite of this a successful merchant trader was determined to increase his trading area into ChapWell Land. Everyone warned him against this, saying only the special Wellian horses were capable of making such a treacherous journey. The merchant asked where he could purchase these horses. Everyone replied the same, 'You cannot, the Wellians keep their horses and never sell the special ones. They only sell those that aren't much good.' The merchant laughed at this and went to the Wellians and asked to buy 20 of their 'special' horses.

The Wellian horse trader refused to sell him the horses. The merchant, being an exceptional trader, carried on cajoling and pleading with the horse trader. Finally the horse trader relented and agreed to loan him 20 Wellian horses in return for a promise. The merchant agreed and the trader said the promise was to bring back the 20 horses having treated them as well as himself. If he failed then the merchant would belong to the Wellian.

The merchant trader agreed and left with the Wellian horses, pleased with the great bargain he had made. He travelled far and wide, all the time loading the Wellian horses with his purchases. The merchant was very pleased with himself, dreaming of the great wealth he would accumulate when the goods were sold. Sure of his great profits, he dined in the best restaurants and stayed in the best hotels.

On the way back five horses became ill due to the cheap food he had bought for them. Sadly the horses became too weak and were sold for a fraction of the price they were worth when he was given them.

Short of horses to carry his fine purchases, the merchant loaded them onto the remaining horses and, grumbling about his profits, carried on. Still, he thought, I could use the money from the horses sold to buy myself a fine meal tonight, and at this thought he felt slightly cheered.

As they travelled on progress was slow and at the next water stop the merchant decided to carry less water for the horses as by now they were all heavily overloaded. Sadly, this didn't help the horses and five more became unable to continue. By the time the merchant reached the last town before the perilous mountain passes there remained only five of the original 20 horses.

The merchant left the horses to forage in the scrubland behind the hotel as he headed into the hotel to refresh himself and drown his sorrows, he thought. Immediately he entered the hotel he saw the Wellian horse trader and accused him of swindling him by selling him weak and feeble horses.

The Wellian trader looked out of the window at the remaining sorry-looking horses and then at the merchant who looked plumper despite the journey. The Wellian trader sighed, shook his head and quietly replied, 'No, you swindled me. You now work for me; I will treat you as well as you treat your horses.'

Chapter 6
The Future in the Now

Key 5 – Use now to create your nows

Dreams are tomorrow's hopes and today's steps towards reality... you choose, create or stagnate.

ChapWellian saying circa 875

Do you know your goals?

Are your goals happening in your today?

Is your attitude aligned with your goals?

Are you enjoying your goals already?

Intentions a pathway to success

Just setting goals is only half the story; you choose your destination and you journey towards it. I soon realised that if we just focus on the goals, they are set in the future and leave us with little for today. I totally agree you need to state your goals in the now, as if they exist, but there's a thing called that little word 'if'. 'If' implies choice and we are talking about a definitive route to creating change, to bringing into being what we really want! I choose to live with intention, making each day an opportunity to bring my goals into reality.

Intentions with attitude

Intentions allow me to create and hold the attitude of having what I want, enjoying the process of creating what I want and feeling that bubble of excitement as each step today gives me a burst of feeling – of what it feels like to have the goal firmly in place.

Excitement and joy

This approach means you get to enjoy all those feelings now of having what you want, with every action, thought and step aligned to your goal power and boosting your goal into the now. You quickly develop a 'can-do' attitude, an attitude that boosts your goal, supporting you through to attracting your goal into your life. Much better than waiting for something to happen. It's here and I'm growing it! Attracting intentions works so much better for me and those I work with, making them realise the journey is as important as the arriving! Just being focused on the goal makes us vulnerable to setbacks and blocks whereas intention helps us learn and enjoy the journey as it prepares us to be fully able to grow and create.

To make this clear, acting with intention doesn't mean acting as if you have achieved the goal, it means that each day you know you will achieve it so you act, plan and prepare. Say for example you want to double your salary. It doesn't mean you start spending double your salary, rather you realise you are already halfway there and look for ways to achieve the other half. Also you would start preparing for what you are going to do with the extra income, say open a savings account to save more, plan out a kitchen redesign; you start knowing that it will happen and the timing is not up to you but the attracting most definitely is! It is called the co-creation process.

Law of attraction

Intentions work brilliantly with the law of attraction. It relies on your ability to create and shift your focus into the direction you want, believe it is possible, affirm it is happening, experience your intention as real and start to create what you want now. Every step you take now is part of the reality of your goal happening. What could be more real than that? Today, now, you have the attitude of experiencing, living and believing your goal is real.
If, however, you choose to allow doubts into your language and thinking, perhaps saying things like hope and try, all you'll create is lots of hope and lots of trying! Your choice!

Divining your goals and therefore your intentions

This is a fantastic tool for divining your goals and making sure you are meeting all of your needs and really want your goal. For example if you decide you want to create more money in your life, you may decide to work longer hours and neglect another important part of your life e.g. your health, wellbeing, family, relationships and so on. Key 5 helps you decide how and what to bring into your life whilst creating a balanced life that meets all your needs. In short it helps you check out your needs against what you think you want!

Check out your wishes

I formed an NLP Practice Group (an opportunity for people to develop, share and practise NLP skills) which was attended by some very experienced NLP Masters right through to those who just wanted to know what NLP was all about. During a discussion about goal setting and finding out what you want one member shared his experience. He had set some goals and set about creating them but, he warned, this stuff really works. He reached his goal, to have plenty of money, but to his cost he had found out it wasn't what he really wanted. Now he had a pile of other problems to solve! So this exercise helps you to check out what is important to you so you can decide what you want and balance your intentions and approach to achieving your goal, aligned with what you desire and need as a whole person.

I suggest you take a light hearted approach to this exercise, despite the dire warning above! Treat life as a jungle journey and one we learn from as we travel. If we relax and allow ourselves to learn along the route we can then make adjustments to suit us as we grow and develop a life more suited to our needs. Isn't it true that a lot of the things we have desired and worked towards may have come about but a major part of the having was the journey we took getting to our goal? That's why the intention is as important as the goal; after all, the achievement of one goal only tends to lead to the setting of another, so intention needs to be a major part of our life.

> Life can be like a wonderful garden. Once the flower has bloomed the wise gardener enjoys the bloom whilst tending the seeds it scatters.
>
> Chapwellian saying 1467

Savour the journey as part of your desires

I was walking with a group just a few days ago. We walked at a good pace and took time to enjoy the beautiful countryside and savour the panoramic views. One of the group remarked that most of his walking was about speed and despite walking in various beautiful spots his pace was so fast he missed the scenery and landscape. I wondered if his intention was to walk or to finish or maybe something else altogether. On talking further it became clear his intention was to keep fit and lose weight. Not very different from my annual 10-15 miles a week to keep fit, but I wondered who got more out of the journey, me or him. My walking gives me loads: relaxation, a step away from my work, friends, fun and companionship, all this as a bonus to keeping fit and being outdoors with nature. If we act in intention we allow life to give us the unexpected bonuses, more than just a goal reached. Why be restricted by our own imagination which is only borne of what we already know; be open and prepared to welcome in all the other things our goal gives us if and when we choose to allow intention to play a part.

Intentions work with the process of change

Remember the change process I mentioned earlier: the stages we go through and recognising relapse as a natural part of change. It's not always present but it occurs frequently. Relapse or reverting to previous behaviours or thinking is not a signal to give up but to check out what you want and adapt your intentions to make it happen. Replan when to practise the change you are working on, and how to make it easier for yourself. A relapse is a mere hiccup, a signal you are changing, otherwise you wouldn't have noticed you have reverted to the previous thinking and behaviours, now would you? It is important to see any change as a process, not a finite thing. Intentions recognise we are unique individuals, allowing you to plan a change and coach yourself through the change process.

Say for example you decide to start using the ChapWell Method as part of your life. So your intention is to include some of the exercises in your daily life and live your days in an increased state of peace and calm.

Here's an example of the change process

Tackle change as a journey

Understanding and approaching change as a process enables you to get to know the best ways for you to tackle a change. For example, you have decided to follow a healthy diet and you start the day with a healthy well balanced diet, take a nutritious lunch with you and then find during the mid-afternoon you are so hungry you are tempted by the chocolate bars in the machine at work. So you have one. You then have a choice – go back to the old eating habits, stay the same, or use this new information about yourself and go back to the 'what's this' or finding out stage of the change process. Find out how you can balance your food intake so you can have something mid-afternoon and avoid the hunger pangs that make it harder for you to stick to the new diet. I have found this approach to change the most productive and so have many of my clients. In fact one client gave up smoking that way. Instead of caving in totally and buying a packet of cigarettes if she succumbed to a puff, she considered it as a signal she was changing. She reviewed her day, carried on living a smoke free day and gradually walked away from smoking cigarettes. In addition she used the tips in Key 7 to support her towards success.

Timing is important

Part of the law of attraction and reaching your goals is all about the timing. Some things we think we have control over when, in truth, we only have control over ourselves. Therefore intentions enable us to plan and prepare for reaching our goal and when the time is right we are ready to allow our goal to come into reality.

Nowadays we often expect things to be immediate, and if they aren't we start to trigger stress. If we form intentions this helps the power of attraction to allow the timing factor to be perfect for us. How many times in your life have you experienced a disappointment or a setback and later realised that what happened next turned that disappointment into a 'good job that happened' situation? Intentions help you to trust, do your bit to make things happen and enjoy the journey.

Exercise – Creating Unique Intentions

Get yourself an intentions book or if you prefer to use IT set up a folder marked 'My intentions' and start creating. First jot down your goals, the things you want to create in your life.

Make sure your intentions follow the absolutes of goal setting too:

- **stated in the Now** – as if you have it now, it exists

- **for you, as an 'I' statement** – totally about what **you** want, no one else

- **in the positive** – only includes what you want

For example

- To keep fit, I enjoy exercising daily. I am strong and healthy. I am confident my body is strong and healthy.

- I complete all my assignments effortlessly and on time.

- I have a wonderful partner who meets all my needs.

- My services are in great demand, I have many clients/customers and a waiting list.

- I only eat healthy food that will keep me strong and slender.

- I easily meet my sales targets one day before the deadline.

- I have 30 minutes' quiet, uninterrupted time each day.

For each goal start to develop and examine their strength in the following way:

Having my goal – write as much as you can so you really understand what you want.

1. I will be ....
....
....

2. It will be important to me because ....
....
....

3. I will know it is right for me because ....
    ....
    ....

4. My goal will enable me to ....
    ....
    ....

5. I can then ....
    ....
    ....

6. I will (do/learn/develop/grow) ....
    ....
    ....

7. I will act in this way...
    ....
    ....

8. How will my days be? Where will I be? What will my surroundings be? ....
    ....
    ....

9. How will this affect those that are important to me? (If it matters to you what others will think or do, then ask them; don't assume you know what others think!) ....
    ....
    ....

10. How do I know these things? ....
    ....
    ....

Mind reading not a success

If your goal will impact on others it is important to find out how they would react, to get them on board and to check that you are OK with how they will react. If you have someone important in your life do not presume to know how they would be if you change, what they would do or what they would think. A goal will mean change, so ask them what they will think, and how they will be affected. When asking others make it clear you are asking them how they would be towards you when your goal starts to take form outwardly, NOT what they think of your goal unless you want their opinion; if so, make that clear too.

Exercise - Installing Your Goals

Have your intention notebook or file beside you, not to use whilst doing this exercise but to refer to immediately after this self-hypnosis exercise. After you have completed the self-hypnosis you can then review your goals and add or even take away what you no longer feel is important to you or part of what you want and need.

Remembering the safety instructions, make sure you are safe to 'go within' and remove your awareness from your surroundings. You can use these instructions to refer to if you need as you take yourself into trance quickly and easily by returning to your 'comfy chair place'.

Key Points

- relaxing both your mind and body

- going to your safe place

- imagine having each goal in place, what you would

- do, feel, be, want

1. Get yourself comfortable and in a safe place where you can go inwards without being disturbed for about 10 to 15 minutes. Keep your answers beside you on your intentions list.

2. **Power Breaths** – Take 3 deep breaths, breathe in to the count of 3, pause and release your breath to the count of 3. Then allow your breathing to settle to normal.

3. Imagine going down your 10 step staircase, through the door into your safe place.

4. Enjoy being in your special, safe place; notice the colours, sounds, smells, the way things are placed, notice shapes and form.

5. When you are ready sink into your 'comfy chair'.

6. Feel that wonderful feeling of relaxation, peace and calm.

7. Staying in your comfy chair, begin to allow your mind to think about your goals.

8. Work through each goal. Ask yourself, is there anything else you need to consider?

9. Now imagine yourself having, being, living your goal. Notice how you feel, how you think, how you act, how you react to others.

10. Work your way through each goal. Make sure you work your way through each of your goals before you do the next exercise. See yourself moving, speaking, interacting with your goal fully in place, and part of you. Ask yourself what you would be doing and imagine doing it.

11. When you are sure you have explored all of the goals you have planned to explore in this hypnosis session, gently move your mind to be aware of your comfy chair, and just relax and enjoy the peace and calm of your safe place. Relax deeply into your comfy chair if you are going into a deep sleep now.

12. If you are getting on with your day, when you are ready leave your 'comfy chair', go through the door and take your 10 steps back into the now.

13. Stretch, blink, make sure you are fully alert before you review your goals list. (If you are doing this exercise before going to sleep do your review when you awake.)

Exercise – Review and Reflect

Immediately after your hypnosis, read through your goal notes and see if it is true for you still, or is there anything you want to add, change or improve?

1. I will be ....
....
....

2. It will be important to me because ....
....
....

3. I will know it is right for me because ....
....
....

4. My goal will bring ....
....
....

5. I can then ....
....
....

6. I will (do/learn/develop/grow) ....
....
....

7. I will act in this way...
....
....

8. I will feel..

....

....

9. How will my days be? Where will I be? What will my surroundings be?..

....

....

10. How will this affect those that are important to me? (if it matters to you what others think then ask them; don't assume you know what others think!) ....

....

....

11. Will it meet my 'must have' needs? ....

....

....

Use this review and reflect process to check you know exactly what you want and that it suits you perfectly. Keep adding to and changing your goal(s) until you decide your goal is detailed enough, clear to you and absolutely right for you now.

Once you have your goal firmly in your mind you can start creating. Here are some tips to help you attract it into your life and experience your intention happening in your life NOW.

Use the 3Ds – Directed Day Dreaming

Whenever you have a moment, allow your mind to wander and daydream what it will be like having your goal. Let your mind enjoy every moment and allow your daydream to really allow you to experience having totally completed your goal. This helps create a can-do mindset and a belief that you can really complete your intention: an inner knowing leading to increased motivation and focus.

Mirror work

Every morning when you are getting yourself ready for your day make sure you take a few moments and look deeply into your eyes in the mirror and repeat your goals. It is best to repeat 3 times to allow the knowledge to sink into your subconscious and support you to complete your goal. You may feel a bit odd doing this but remember the subconscious is very black and white and believes what it is told. If you believe it you can create it. This exercise helps you strengthen your self-belief.

Write or word process

Use your intention log book or file to write out your goal(s) on a daily basis. This helps keep them firmly in your consciousness and pushed onwards towards your long-term memory. Regularly writing your goals down allows you to see opportunities and options as they come up to speed your progress to completion.

Maybe you have heard the urban myth about the Harvard or Yale University students who wrote down their goals and were more successful than those who did not write down their goals. Well that study did happen but it was conducted by Gail Matthews, PhD, at Dominican University with 149 students. So there is proof that goals and intentions benefit from being written down and success increases still further if you also include a friend as a supporter and someone who you can give regular reports on your progress to!

Use self-hypnosis

Regularly tap into your inner wisdom and discuss your intentions with your older self. Use the 'Tapping into Your Wisdom' exercise in chapter 5 as an opportunity to explore, gain support, report progress, problem solve and gain guidance. When visiting your comfy chair enjoy imagining having your goal as part of your life.

Tap into your personal power

Use the self-hypnosis exercises to help you tap into your personal power and increase your success. If you need more energy, confidence, focus or something else, the exercises in Key 6 can help you access and transfer those important ways of being at the time and place to support you. One of my clients assured me that she didn't have any confidence. I asked her if she was confident when she cleaned her teeth. Of course, she replied. I then explained that she had confidence; she just needed to be able to access it at all the times she wanted confidence, not just when it happened to show up!

Remove the barriers to your success

Sometimes patterns, old learning and ways of thinking no longer work in our now and in fact cause the very problems we are trying to resolve. Key 7 includes some basic methods to help you develop and create new ways of thinking and easier ways of tackling problems – the barriers to your success.

Treat the leaves to keep the blossom free of disease or treat the roots so the tree is strong, spreads its branches, continues to grow and blossoms again and again.

ChapWellian saying circa 1275

Chapter 7
Magnificent Personal Power

Key 6 – Feed your need mores

So just reflect for a moment now that you can

- Achieve a peaceful, calm and relaxed state in just a thought, a thought of your 'comfy chair'.

- Enjoy living in the now.

- Clear away your negative thought patterns and replace them with thoughts that accelerate you towards success, happiness and wellbeing.

- Create goals and intentions aligned with the uniqueness of you and what you really want to create.

Draw on your wonderful powers – tap into what you need when you need it!

Need more energy?

Need more confidence?

Need more concentration?

Need more motivation?

Need more ... whatever you choose?

What could you, would you do or be if you could easily power boost your performance?

You have already learnt how to install and train your mind to effortlessly choose peace and calm through the 'comfy chair' exercise. It naturally follows that you can choose other ways of 'being' to suit what you are doing, need and want to achieve. Using the simple techniques you have now mastered, all can be done using your 'comfy chair' in peace and calm. So why wouldn't you?

Enjoy the journey as well as the destination

Just as you have trained your mind to summon up calm and peace in a thought, you can easily train your mind to give you that extra confidence, the focus that gets things done, that energy and enthusiasm to keep on going towards your goals and enjoy the journey as well as the achievement. Living your life in a way that enables you and helps you enjoy the experience of your jungle journey as well as the achievement. After all, the journey is what life is all about, isn't it?

Your personal power

Understand you have everything you need ready for you to draw on your personal power and talents when and where you need them. Need more energy? Need more confidence? Need more motivation? Need more concentration? Whatever 'state' you need you can transfer those actions, feelings and thoughts to enable you to bring it into the now! Have you ever heard yourself say 'I wish

I had more patience' or 'I wish I had more energy' or 'I wish I had more confidence' or 'I wish I had more focus, concentration, willpower' and so on and on?

Get started

The important thing is to recognise what you want and then recognise you already have it – either by imagining or by recalling a time when you were fully in that state. Just a reminder, by 'state' I mean the way you felt, acted and thought. Imagining works just as powerfully on the subconscious as it a strong part of your mind that accepts what it is told, so long as there isn't a conflict with an instruction already given, sometimes unwittingly by us!

Let your imagination work for you

You can either imagine what you would be like, what you would do, how you would be or act as if you had what you think you need. Or pick a time when you have been in the state you want (confident, energetic, motivated and so on) and use that as your example. You can access the state you want (from a real or imagined example), take a copy and build a set of easy channels in your mind, like a TV set, to effortlessly bring into your now what you need. Once the state is installed you can then access more of what you want by just switching to the channel in your mind. Remember you are always in charge and you can easily access and use all your talents and gifts, so why don't you?

Exercise - Energy Installer

As usual make sure you are safe to 'switch off' from the outside world for about 20 to 30 minutes. Either lie down or get yourself comfortable in a chair. Switch off phones and any other potential distractions as much as you can. If you choose to do this one before you go to sleep make sure you stay in your comfy chair and allow time for that feeling of relaxation, peace and calm to send you off to sleep. So first get yourself comfortable.

Key points

- Power Breaths

- Comfy chair

- Imagine a TV screen

- Switch on your energy channel

- Visualise you at your most energetic

- Step into your energetic self

- At your most energetic step out

- Return to the comfy chair

- Repeat

- Return to the now full of energy

1. Power Breaths – Breathe in counting 1, 2, 3, pause and out 3, 2, 1, pause. Do this for 6 to 12 breaths.

2. As you breathe allow your eyes to close.

3. Allow your body to relax.

4. Now imagine yourself going down the 10 step stairway and opening the door into your safe place.

5. Look around your safe place for a few minutes and enjoy that feeling of calm and peace.

6. When you are ready sit yourself in your comfy chair and let that feeling of peace and calm wrap itself around you like a warm blanket.

7. Continue to enjoy that feeling of total relaxation, calm and peace in your very own place. Allow the feeling to grow and envelop you like a warm blanket.

8. When you feel yourself totally relaxed notice a large TV screen in front of you.

9. Switch on the screen and see a channel listing on the screen. Imagine and select the channel marked 'Energy'. However you choose to switch on the screen and select the energy channel is good; maybe you'll give it a number or a coloured

button. Just make sure you'll know; remember what switch turns on your energy channel. Accept whatever your mind gives you.

10. Watch the picture emerge, a picture of you at your most energetic, most alert, full of energy, supple, full of life, laughing with loads of energy, just bubbling with energy.

11. Enjoy watching yourself on the screen noticing how energetic, strong and alert you are. Enjoy watching yourself in this state. Maybe it is from a past time or maybe it is imagined; both are fine for this exercise. Just make sure you know it is you. Believe and understand that this is you at your most energetic. Continue to relax and enjoy watching yourself fully alert, full of mental and physical energy, enjoying yourself, full of life, moving with ease and energy, confidently completing all tasks, full of energy and eager for the next thing.

12. Put lots of colour into the picture of yourself and when you can feel, hear or see yourself nearing your peak energy levels, step into the screen, into your body and enjoy the feelings, sensations and sounds you hear; enjoy the feel of yourself, full of physical and mental energy.

13. Really feel being this 'energetic you', continuing to experience the energy build and build in you.

Enjoy being yourself at your peak physical and mental energy levels. Enjoy experiencing your energetic feelings, your energetic thoughts, your energetic actions.

14. When you know and feel you are at your peak energy levels, imagine stepping out of the screen. Then switch off your energy channel using your energy button or switch. Notice how the screen goes blank.

15. Relax deeply into your comfy chair and enjoy the peace, calm and relaxed feeling that sitting in your safe place gives you.

16. Let that feeling of relaxation and peace wash over you.

17. Now switch on the screen in front of you and again select your energy channel.

18. As the picture comes on immediately step into the screen.

19. Feel yourself full of energy. Enjoy those energetic thoughts, actions and feelings immediately you step into the screen. Now step out of the screen taking all those feelings with you. Enjoy walking around your safe place full of energy.

20. When you are ready to leave go through your door and up the stairs.

21. Come back into the now bringing all those energetic feelings with you.

22. Stretch, yawn and blink bringing yourself to full alertness. As usual do not carry on with your day until you are fully awake and alert.

You are now tapping into your personal powers, moving them around to suit you, all from the comfort of your relaxation and peaceful chair. Now having set a direct channel to boost your energy levels, over the next few days you need to tune in to your energy channel to boost the connection, just as you did to boost your connection to peace and calm through your 'comfy chair'. Exactly as you have established the ability to experience calm and relaxation by a thought, you will now do the same with energy. Once you have fully boosted and secured your energy channel you can then easily tap into an energy boost with just a thought of switching on or pressing the button to your energy channel. It's very useful to able to effortlessly tap into an energy boost when you need it, I'm sure we'll all admit to that, and far better than reaching for caffeine or sugar to give us that boost. It may be you will use it at the end of a busy day when you need to do a few more things before you rest. It may be when you are feeling low and just cannot seem to get yourself going, whenever you choose. So long as you keep the connection boosted, you will be able to tap into this energy store to suit you.

Over the next few days strengthen your ability to channel into your Energy source

Strengthen your energy channel by repeating the longer exercise, really boosting that energetic experience. Use the following exercise to find out when it is fully boosted and firmly connected. Once you can access your energy source quickly using the exercise below you know you have fully installed access to your energy boost and can just use the exercise below when you need it!

Exercise – Mini Energy Boost

Key Points

- **Power Breaths**

- **Comfy chair**

- **Switch on your energy channel**

- **Step into the screen**

- **Feel the energy build**

- **Leave the screen taking your energy with you**

- **Return to your now**

As usual make sure you are safe to 'switch off' from the outside world for about 5 minutes.

1. Get yourself comfortable

2. **Power Breaths** – Breathe in counting 1, 2, 3, pause and out 3, 2, 1, pause. Do this for 3–6 breaths.

3. Allow your eyes to close.

4. Imagine you are sitting in your 'comfy chair'; feel that relaxation, calm and peace surround you like a warm blanket.

5. Notice your screen in front of you. Switch on your screen to your energy channel and quickly step into the screen. Immediately feel and experience that energetic state you have created.

6. Allow yourself to absorb that energy until you are experiencing your peak energy state.

7. As you step out of the screen take your peak energy state with you and come back into the now. Open your eyes, blink, stretch. Feel your high energy levels and carry on with what you need to do once you are fully alert.

Major to mini

I use this mini booster whenever I need some extra energy to carry out a task, or on a day when my batteries are feeling a bit flat. Or when I am working out and looking for that extra energy to keep going to the end. The more you tune in to your energy channel the stronger it will become. A bit like the workout adage, 'Use it or lose it'. You have done the work through the longer Energy Boost Exercise, now use it to reap the benefits and enjoy!

Remember balance

Treat yourself kindly though; remember that if you notice you are boosting yourself like this through the day, it may mean you are not getting enough rest anyway. Or, if you are like me, you sometimes have a lot of work to do and need to meet the deadlines. In this case I try to make sure that after the deadline has been met I make sure I give myself enough rest and relaxation to recharge my batteries properly. If you need an energy boost I am sure you know the reason why – late nights or broken, sleepless nights – so promise to give yourself some boosters of relaxation using your 'virtual chair' or an early night or whatever it is you'll need. Do whatever you need to restore your energy levels to normal. Remember the tale of the Wellian horses, and make sure you are taking care of your horse – you!

Route map

The important thing to understand is that by the repeating of the longer self-hypnosis energy exercise you are building a highway to your energy store so you can draw on extra when needed. Then you can trigger an energy boost easily and effortlessly when you need it. I wonder how many times you have thought or said, 'This would be OK if I wasn't feeling so tired'. Or something similar. Well, now you can make it OK.

Energy – just a moment away

Use the Energy Boost to maximise your performance and remember, relaxation of the mind feeds and nurtures it as well, and is crucial to releasing the wonderful powers you have! This is about using your power to maintain a clear healthy mind, body and emotions. Just like a beautiful machine you need to make sure you rest it as well as turn it up to peak performance. I have found through my own experience that to allow peace and calm to become your default setting is a wonderful basis for rising to all the challenges of the day. You can still be energetic and retain a peaceful mindset and in fact it makes your energy more sustainable and avoids what I call the sugar rush syndrome, when you have a burst of energy and then feel more depleted of energy than before you began. By continuing to boost calm and peace through regular flash thoughts of your 'comfy chair', your peace and calm store, your default setting very quickly becomes peace and calm – lovely!!!

And there's more than energy …

You can now set up quick fire channels to the boost you need. All you need to do is insert the thoughts, emotions and actions you want to boost in yourself so that you can give yourself a super boost whenever you feel you need it. Remember how you set up your channel to the 'state' you wanted through the deeper self-hypnosis exercise of 20 to 30 minutes and then just a couple of minutes checking each day until your channel is a direct highway to whatever state you want. After a short while you will find you are 'hardwired' for whichever channels you have tuned yourself into and they are now part of your magnificent support team – YOU. I frequently draw on different states to make sure I have the right mindset and state for my needs or the tasks I need to complete. If I want more energy I just programme it in (I did that years ago) and now as I need it I just flip my energy channel on for a minute and give myself the boost I need. Easy to do and all from a place of relaxation and calm!

Here's another example to help you get well and truly into power boosting. You will know what you need and it is easy for you to use this exercise to achieve exactly what you need and want. Just change energy or confidence for the power boost you want and follow the rest of the instructions!

Exercise - Confidence Installer: Setting a channel to boost your confidence

As usual make sure you are safe to 'switch off' from the outside world for about 20 to 30 minutes. Either lie down or get yourself comfortable in a chair. Switch off phones and any other potential distractions as much as you can. If you choose to do this one before you go to sleep make sure you stay in your comfy chair and allow time for that feeling of relaxation, peace and calm to send you off to sleep. So first get yourself comfortable.

Key points

- **Power Breaths**

- **Comfy chair**

- **Imagine a TV screen**

- **Switch on your confidence channel**

- **Visualise you at your most confident**

- **Step into your confident self**

- **At your most confident step out**

- **Return to the comfy chair**

- **Repeat**

- **Return to the now full of confidence**

1. Power Breaths – Breathe in counting 1, 2, 3, pause and out 3, 2, 1, pause. Do this for 6 to 12 breaths.

2. As you breathe allow your eyes to close.

3. Allow your body to relax.

4. Now imagine yourself going down the 10 step stairway and opening the door into your safe place.

5. Look around your safe place for a few minutes and enjoy that feeling of calm and peace.

6. When you are ready sit yourself in your comfy chair.

7. Continue to enjoy that feeling of total relaxation, calm and peace in your very own place. Allow the feeling to grow and envelop you like a warm blanket.

8. When you feel yourself totally relaxed notice a large TV screen in front of you.

9. Switch on the screen and see a channel listing on the screen. Select the channel marked 'Confidence'. As before, however you choose to switch on the screen and select the confidence channel is fine.

10. Watch the picture emerge, a picture of you at your most confident, most assured, full of confidence, smiling, calm, poised, whatever confidence looks like, sounds like, feels like for you. Watch yourself move with confidence, talk to others, laugh, smile, say the absolute right things, move in the absolutely right way, dressed confidently, full of confidence, surrounded by approving people.

11. Enjoy watching yourself on the screen noticing how confident, self-assured, relaxed and at ease you are. Enjoy watching yourself in this ultra-confident state. Maybe it is from a past time or maybe it is imagined, or maybe it is the situation you want to feel and be more confident in; whatever you choose is good. Just make sure you know it is you. Believe and understand that this is you at your

most confident, successful and self-assured, easy with yourself and all those around you. Continue to relax and enjoy watching yourself fully alert, full of confidence, self-assurance and at ease, moving with ease and confidence, confidently completing all tasks knowing it is easy for you. Knowing all is well and you are well suited for all situations that come your way. Knowing you are good enough and all is well with you.

12. Put lots of colour in the picture of yourself and when you can feel, hear and see yourself nearing your peak confidence levels, step into the screen, into your body and enjoy the feelings, sensations, sounds you hear, enjoy the feel of yourself, full of physical and mental confidence. Enjoy feeling full of confidence, moving with confidence, thinking, smiling and talking confidently, enjoying carrying out whatever you are doing.

13. Enjoy being this confident you; continue to experience the confidence building in you, knowing all is well and you are perfectly suited and capable for whatever life holds for you. Enjoy being yourself at your peak confidence and wellbeing levels and then double the feelings, thoughts and actions in confidence. Enjoy experiencing your feelings of confidence, your confident thoughts, your confident actions and movements.

14. When you feel you are at your peak confidence levels, step out of the screen, switch off your confidence channel and notice how the screen goes blank.

15. Relax into your comfy chair and enjoy the peace, calm and relaxed feeling sitting in your safe place gives you.

16. Let that feeling of relaxation and peace wash over you.

17. Now switch on the screen in front of you and again select your confidence channel.

18. As the picture comes on immediately step into the screen and into yourself.

19. Feel yourself full of confidence. Enjoy those confident thoughts, actions and feelings immediately you step into the screen. Now step out of the screen taking all those feelings, ways of moving, ways of thinking with confidence with you. Enjoy walking around your safe place full of confidence.

20. When you are ready to leave go through your door and up the 10 step staircase.

21. Come back into the now when you are ready.

22. Stretch, yawn and blink bringing yourself back to being fully alert.

Easy access

Over the next few days strengthen your ability to channel into your confidence source Strengthen your confidence channel by repeating the longer exercise, really boosting that confidence source. Use the following exercise to check for when it is fully boosted and firmly connected. Once you can access your confidence source quickly using the exercise below, you know you have fully installed access to your confidence boost and can simply use the exercise below when you need it!

Exercise – Mini Confidence Boost

Key Points

- **Power Breaths**

- **Comfy chair**

- **Switch on your energy channel**

- **Step into the screen**

- **Feel the energy build**

- **Leave the screen taking your energy with you**

- **Return to your now**

As usual make sure you are safe to 'switch off' from the outside world for about 5 minutes.

1. Get yourself comfortable.

2. **Power Breaths** – Breathe in counting 1, 2, 3, pause and out 3, 2, 1, pause. Do this for 3 to 6 breaths.

3. Allow your eyes to close.

4. Imagine you are sitting in your 'comfy chair'; feel that relaxation, calm and peace surround you like a warm blanket.

5. Notice your screen in front of you. Switch on your screen to your confidence channel and quickly step into the screen. Immediately feel and experience that confident state you have created.

6. Allow yourself to absorb those confident feelings, ways of moving and thinking until you are experiencing your peak confident state.

7. Taking your peak confidence state with you, come back into the now. Open your eyes, blink, stretch. Feel your high levels of confidence and carry on with what you need to do once you are fully alert.

Major to mini

Use the mini booster whenever you need some extra confidence, the same way as you use it for an energy boost. The same principle applies for the energy channel; the more you tune in to your confidence channel the stronger it will become. On my one-day courses we usually focus on just one booster and install it first thing in the morning, again at midday and by the end of the day do the mini exercise and find it is in place. It seems to then work best if over the next week delegates carry out the longer exercise one more time and access the booster through the mini exercise 4 or 5 times over the next week. Obviously for some the installing and accessing their energy or confidence boost will be much quicker but I am just giving you an idea of the set-up time.

Lifetime installation

Having installed your energy and confidence boosters they will be there for you so long as you use them. Frequently clients forget to use them and through lack of use they may become weaker. All you need to do is use them to keep them strong once installed and enjoy the benefits. If you don't use your confidence or energy boosts you may think you have lost them but by just redoing the exercise you will find your extra booster source. You'll always have the booster sources available to you, even before doing the exercise you have just forgotten or don't yet know how to find it. Better still the more you use it the stronger it becomes. Remember you now have these wonderful boosters available to you so get used to enjoying them! I use beads to prompt me, to remind me that I have tools I can use to make my day, all of the ups and downs and in-betweens, work beautifully for me. You can find your own prompter but I suggest you do, otherwise, especially in the early days, you may forget to access what you need. Falling back on old habits is easy and part of the change process is to notice when you do this, so choose a prompt! Maybe your prompt will be every time you do something, like have a drink, or eat, take off your shoes, sit down, I leave it up to you to choose.

Add in more channels to suit YOU

Use the same longer and mini booster exercises to bring in more channels of whatever you want more of for your jungle journey. All you need to do is replace the state with the one you want; instead of imagining yourself in an energetic or confident state imagine the state you want and set up another 'switch on' button, easily adding to the channels available to you. As time goes on and your installed states become stronger, all you will need to do is switch your channel on and you will have more of what you want.

Choose happiness

I have focused on energy and confidence as examples as they are ones people frequently ask me for in sessions, mainly because I include happiness in my courses as standard! So don't forget to install happiness using the same technique!

Chapter 8
Your Jungle Freedom

Key 7 – Sweep aside the barriers

Do you have similar problems or recurring themes in your life?

Do you ask yourself why me ... again?

Do you get only so far with something before you start to experience roadblocks?

Is there always someone in your life that causes you problems?

Do your relationships follow a similar pattern?

Do you suffer from aches and pains?

Some easy sweeps

If we have a problem, physical or mental, it makes sense to do something about it – why live with it? So rather than put up with whatever is bothering you, it makes sense to get some expert help and get it sorted. However, often there is a lot we can do for ourselves if we knew how! Most of us know how to support our physical wellbeing: good diet, plenty of exercise and rest, and when necessary to promptly seek and follow expert medical help. Often we forget that our mental wellbeing is important too and something we can easily support and maintain for ourselves. It never ceases to amaze me how frequently people will take seriously their responsibility to keep themselves physically well and see a relevant expert practitioner if they need help, but they do not consider the same approach with their minds. Maybe if we learnt in schools how we have the ability to direct our minds, how to keep them well, balanced and working for us, and when to seek expert help to assist us in looking after our mental health, the incidence of stress-related illnesses would be reduced – just maybe!

Easy useful tools

Using the tools in this book you now have some very useful tools to promote your wellbeing, by directing your mind to support you and work for you. So I thought it would be useful to add some optional extras from the wide range I cover on my courses to support you as the director of your mind and your life. Consider them some extra vitamins for the mind that some of us will benefit from some of the time! I use all of them in my one-to-one coaching practice when needed and I have developed some that you can easily use by yourself. These are tools that help you to continue to take responsibility for your mental wellbeing, keeping your mind healthy and well supported with its equivalent of a good diet, rest and exercise.

What are you feeding your mind?

So often we let our minds dwell on things we cannot change: things from the past, hurts, disappointments and injustices. Or maybe we have learnt to worry, overthink things and look for the negative in things, therefore interpreting the 'now' through a lens of the past. The past is over and cannot be changed but we sometimes keep past events alive in our minds by making sure we continue to feel the emotions, keeping them real and using our wonderful imaginations to make sure they stay fresh and present in our now.

Are you keeping alive the good stuff or the bad?

Worse still, we store them up and if any situation arises that seems (to our minds) to have similarities to that past hurt, slight, disappointment or put-down, we automatically react with the emotions from that past experience. This is like a programme we now run to misguidedly protect ourselves from a repeat experience that was unhappy. Unfortunately the reverse happens! We immediately get in touch with the emotions, thinking patterns and behaviours of the past experience and start to recreate it in this NEW situation. This robs us of our ability to view each situation as it really is, to choose how to respond to the situation and what actions to take.

I worked with a client who experienced a very destructive relationship in her early twenties and had gone on, in her words, 'to pick rubbish partners' from there on in. Her reaction to any relationship that was not working had been to leave and now in her fifties she had three failed marriages behind her and was considering leaving her fourth marriage. When we talked she admitted she still felt very angry at her first partner for treating her so badly and very angry at herself for letting it happen. When I asked her what she would do if she no longer felt this anger and hurt she looked at me blankly and started crying. After some more work she realised that she had been basing her decisions on the anger and hurt she felt from the past, thus keeping the past alive in herself and her external world. After working to clear the anger and hurt, her health and energy levels increased tremendously and her sense of wellbeing flourished. Yes, there was a happy ending: she's still married and happily so, and is, as she put it, 'Finding out about my life through clear glasses'.

We all have ups and downs

Unfortunately in life bad things happen and disappointments are part of life as much as happiness and success. The major factor between a successful life and a struggling life is making sure you clear your negative emotions so those emotions do not provide filters for your today, tomorrow and the next day. Think of Richard Branson: he didn't just arrive in the world successful; he experienced many setbacks in business before he 'made it'. If he had chosen to hang onto the hurt and disappointment of failure you would be thinking 'Richard Who?'. It is our free choice whether we choose to stay stuck in our minds or be truly able to allow new opportunities and new possibilities using the learning from our past or living the learning from our past.

Not forgetting, just learning and releasing the emotions

Your choice ... what do you choose?

To clear away any negative emotions from your past and hang onto the valuable lessons you have learnt so you can create and maximise all opportunities, or maybe keep reliving your past emotions and replicating the same mistakes, just different people, different place, different time?

Become self-aware and self-directing

This is an important tool for you; it is your early warning signal to make sure your thoughts, feelings or actions suit you, what you want, and how you want to be. If you find yourself in a challenging situation you can use Power Breaths to boost and focus or maybe think of your 'comfy chair' and switch your mind into a state of peace and calm. You may choose to draw on a power boost channel too to give you what you need so you can deal effectively, calmly and peacefully with the situation.

Later you can start questioning your thoughts, responses and emotional reactions by applying these questions:

- What did I feel when ...?

- Then what did I think when ...?

- How did I act when ...?

- Were these helpful reactions?

- Did they make me feel better equipped with the challenge?

Just answer the questions and jot down your answers. DO NOT bother with 'because' and never bother with 'why' in this exercise. 'Why' just encourages us to defend and justify our reactions and responses. You can ask the why later to see if there is anything to learn, **NOT** to justify your feelings. Look back at your answers if there is any hint of justification for example because … and then he/she …

This next exercise helps you clear up those emotions that get in your way and stop you thinking clearly, so that you can easily act in the now rather than allowing emotional responses from previous experiences to dictate your now. You'll know when you need to clear things up!!! Remember, change one of our operating triangle (thoughts, emotions and actions) and the others will follow.

Exercise - Clear the Roadblocks

Get to know the grown-up you and how to nurture yourself. You can use this exercise to clear any tension when you have had a tough time or found yourself experiencing negative emotions during your day. I also recommend you do a clearing in each area on a regular basis to keep yourself fit and strong mentally. It's up to you; you'll work out what suits you best, if you experiment.

Choose one of these to work on, just choose any one you want and feel attracted to start with, or maybe choose one of the emotions you experienced today. I recommend you do one at a time, just before you go to sleep or at your favourite time and space for doing the self-hypnosis exercises. If you are hesitating over which one to work with then choose resistance: easy, isn't it? Resistance pops up when you find yourself reacting against something, either doing the exercise (as in this case), choosing one from the list, maybe you looked at the exercise and thought, not for me?

That's what I call resistance.

- **Hurt**

- **Forgiveness**

- **Resistance**

- **Anger**

- **Fear**

- **Jealousy**

- **Guilt**

As usual make sure you are safe to 'switch off' from the outside world for at least 20 to 30 minutes. For this exercise example I am using resistance, just insert the one you want to work on in place of resistance if you have chosen another from the list.

Get yourself comfortable either lying down or sitting.

Key Points

- **Power Breaths**

- **Comfy chair**

- **Imagine your time line**

- **Travel back over your past**

- **Identify resistance spots**

- **Travel back to the now clearing resistance spots**

1. **Power Breaths** – Breathe in counting 1, 2, 3, pause and out 3, 2, 1, pause. Repeat for 3 to 6 breaths and allow your breathing to relax as you feel yourself relaxing.

2. Imagine yourself going down your 10 step staircase and into your safe place. Remember you are totally safe. Enjoy that feeling of relaxation and calm as you enjoy your own personal space.

3. Feel the wonderful feeling of relaxation and peace flow through your body. Relax into your comfy chair. Feel your body being supported by your chair and for a few moments enjoy that feeling of relaxation as you sink deeper into your chair.

4. Now imagine your chair is placed on a line that represents your life. This is your timeline. Imagine that where your chair is now is the now of your timeline. Your future is before you and your past is behind you. Look at your future timeline and then glance at your past timeline. If any of your line is twisted or jumbled just straighten it out. Look at your future timeline disappearing far into the distance in front of you and then look at your past timeline disappearing into the distance behind you.

5. Relax and bring your mind back to the now and feel yourself sink deeper into your comfy chair knowing you are totally safe. Enjoy that feeling of peace, calm and relaxation and imagine wrapping it around you like a warm blanket.

6. Now imagine your chair rises up above your timeline until you can look down on your now. Remind yourself you are totally safe and enjoy this floating feeling as you feel relaxed and calm.

7. In a moment, when you are ready, look back to your past timeline. Ask your mind to show you where resistance is in your timeline. Allow your chair to gently take you back over your past timeline, keeping you high above your timeline. Look for any areas or signs of resistance. Accept the image your mind gives you to represent resistance. It may be pulsing dots, or colours or something else

on your timeline. However your mind chooses to mark out resistance is good. Trust your mind to do what you uniquely need.

8. If at any point you start feeling any resistance in your mind, emotions or body just allow your 'comfy chair' to raise you up higher above your timeline until the feelings or thoughts are gone. Then keep travelling back until you have seen all the resistance in your past. Allow your mind to take you, relax and enjoy the journey, high up above your past timeline marking out all of the resistance spots.

9. If your mind does not seem to give you anything just go with it and accept it is the nature of resistance. It is the intention that works. So no excuses or reasons to analyse or overthink this! As I have said before, this 'overthinking' is just a clever human technique to avoid or resist the work needed!

10. When you feel you have travelled far enough, check you have reached your first marker for resistance, if not keep travelling back until you know you have reached your very first marker for resistance in your past. Now allow your chair to travel a little past that first marker for resistance and look down on it.

11. Remind yourself you wish to keep the learning from resistance and remove all of the emotion.

12. Remember if at any point you start to feel any emotions or thoughts of resistance just raise your chair up higher until the feelings or thoughts have gone.

13. Ask yourself how you can clear away and cleanse all of the resistance markers from your past. Allow your mind to tell you how to clear out and cleanse all of the resistance points in your past timeline. Use whatever your mind gives you.

14. Start travelling back and as you go make sure you clear and cleanse all of the resistance spots/markers before you travel over them. Go at your own pace; just make sure you are thorough. Enjoy the process of clearing away all of the resistance spots on your past timeline.

15. Remember if at any point you start to feel any emotions or thoughts of resistance just raise your chair up higher until the feelings or thoughts have gone.

16. Continue travelling back to the now clearing all of the resistance feelings and thoughts from your past, going as slowly as you need to.

17. Remember you are totally safe in your relaxing, comfy chair so enjoy the journey back to the now.

18. When you reach your now, take a moment to look back at your timeline and notice how clear it is of resistance markers and all those emotions and thoughts.

19. Now look forward into the future, and feel the relaxation, peace and calm your comfy chair gives you.

20. Notice how clear, bright and sparkly your future looks, full of good things. Use your imagination to double the brightness of your now and future timeline.

21. Bring your attention back to you sitting in your comfy chair and how relaxed, calm and at peace you feel in your chair. Allow yourself to safely descend down onto your timeline in the now. Look around and enjoy being in your safe place. Continue to enjoy the peace and calm of this moment.

22. When you are ready return to your now. Stretch, yawn, blink and **give yourself time to become fully alert before you carry on with your day.**

23. If you are doing this exercise just before you settle to sleep just allow yourself to stay in your comfy chair in your safe place until you fall asleep.

Choose to lose the baggage

Carry on working through the list of emotions in the same way as you did with resistance. Just clear those emotions you feel or maybe think are important for you to clear up from your past by inserting the emotion you want to work on instead of 'resistance'.

Avoid repacking your baggage

Once you have cleared out those emotions it is important to make sure your 'now' experiences do not allow you to reinstall negative emotions. So the next exercise enables you to clear any negative emotions and thoughts when, well, let's just say you've had a less than inspiring day! Just to be clear, you are keeping the memories and any learning from your experience. This self-hypnosis just helps you clear away those unhelpful emotions linked to the memory; you experienced them once and there is little to be gained if you keep bringing them back into all your nows. It is the nature of human thinking to review the past, however it can stop us from living in the now and experiencing the now. Bringing negative emotions into our now will drag down our mood and wellbeing.

Escape from the last straw syndrome!

Let's deal with the small stuff first. You know all those little niggling things building up and chipping away at your wellbeing, well that is how it feels anyway? Have you ever overslept and then spent the whole day trying to catch up, deal with minor irritations and generally ended up with a less than good day?

Or was everything going OK and then you made a mistake, or missed an appointment, or dropped milk all over the floor, or someone blamed you unfairly, misunderstood you, or you got stuck in traffic, or queued for longer than you wanted? Have you ever used any of these situations to lift your mood or do you allow your mind to run riot and secure a low mood? Sometimes our moods get so low we finally lose our patience, maybe even react angrily and probably cause bigger problems in our life than all the niggles put together. Do you recognise yourself here? I hope by now you get my point here but let me just ask you one more question. Have you ever used any of these situations as your signal to boost your mood, feelings, thoughts and actions upwards? Upwards to feeling good, to coping magnificently, to just dealing with stuff and leaving it in the past where it belongs?

Break the bad day habit

Why make a bad day worse by giving it a negative filter? Yes, we can all have days when something or maybe more than one thing does not work out as expected or hoped. Resist the urge to make it worse by helping your mood go down. Yes, you can direct your mood, thoughts and emotions, so start directing them UP.

Let me explain a bit more. Most of us have learnt how to react to things going wrong from our parents, carers, teachers, whoever showed us how to react to things going wrong. It follows you then find yourself on a downward mood and spend the day looking for things to reinforce your mood, and justify your negative mindset. Start listening to the words you use: do they lift you up or keep you down?

Start making sure everything you say has a positive spin; your mind is listening and will react accordingly.

I'm not saying things don't matter when they do to you. I'm saying it is important to help yourself to stay positive and spin things in an upward spiral; you can choose irritations and an irritated mood or just stuff that happens and a good mood.

I constantly hear people say things like:

- I'm unlucky

- Why does it always happen to me?

- That's typical

- It's best to expect the worst and then you won't be disappointed

- Today's just going from bad to worse

Spinning Positive

Your conscious and subconscious is listening when you speak, so make sure you only feed it the best diet. Break the habit of speaking in the negative. Move out of the way of negative people; don't even bother arguing, just move on. Negativity is contagious just as positivity is, so which would you rather catch?

Learn to spin your thinking into the positive. Stop and think before you speak, rephrase what you were saying and give it a positive spin instead of a negative spin.

When I started spinning positive I found the words were out before I'd thought. That is just fine; just rephrase whatever you said and carry on.

For example

I'm unlucky. – I am lucky and I let someone else have the luck too.

Why does it always happen to me? – My turn today as I'm special!

That's typical. – Nice to know some things can be relied on. It's best to expect the worst and then you won't be disappointed. – It's best to enjoy the good things when they come along!

Today's just going from bad to worse. – Today's brought a mixed bag, some good and some not so good!

These are just my Positive Spins on the negatives and they allow me to see whatever challenges that come in a positive light and then choose how to react or act. They help set your mood into a can-do mood and enable you to think clearly, not running ahead and worrying about what else, what next and so on.

Try 'Spinning Positive': just start listening to the messages you give out to the universe, to others and most importantly to yourself. Remember what you say helps create your emotions, thoughts and actions and dictates your mood. So learn to spin positive; it doesn't change what is but helps your mind and self to realise, 'It's OK! I can cope great, no problem'.

Added attraction

Whether you believe in the law of attraction or not there is one law that works beautifully here. Positive people attract positive people to them. I have heard, seen and witnessed this advice to make friends and get along with colleagues: get them talking about themselves and to make them remember you, spin positive. It's true. If you're lonely, want to attract more people in your life or just fit in with a particular group, listen more and spin positive. So as you learn how to 'Spin Positive' you will find that people are attracted to you, want to be in your company, and want to spend time with you. Opportunities, options and possibilities start to blossom in your life as your life expands and your thinking doesn't drag you down into a worrying, negative pattern.

Remind yourself of the good things

When things are sad and not going well it can be very hard not to add to your burden, instead of just accepting and allowing things to exist whilst you readjust. When my husband died it was very hard at times to function. So I decided to make sure that every hour I did something good; some days it was every 30 minutes and I set my alarm to remind myself. That ranged from reading a favourite silly poem, standing in the winter sunshine for a few moments, looking in the mirror and smiling, and stopping and listing everything that had gone smoothly so far that day. My list went like this: my alarm woke me, the electric worked, hot water for my shower, sweet-smelling soap and so on. Not big things but things that reminded me all was going OK. I even made sure I saw my tears as a positive, good, allowing myself to let go of a bit of sadness by crying it away.

So often people beat themselves up for crying and see it as weakness; it's not, it's our way of expressing and releasing sadness, disappointment and all those other emotions. Crying only becomes a problem when it happens at inappropriate times, times we don't feel we 'should be' crying. These break-out times can be a result of trying to suppress our emotions rather than work our way through them by first accepting them, clearing them (crying is nature's way) and then leaving them behind.

It's simple to make those 'not so good days' into rich days where you can really start to feel the amazing benefits of your ability to direct your mind and your experience and turn things around.

Exercise - Music to Clear Niggles Exercise

This is a quick and easy way to clear unhelpful emotions. I am talking about the memory of something you did or said that made you wish the ground would swallow you up! Or the bad presentation you did at work or maybe you forgot something or someone and now you feel bad. Those times when our mind likes to dwell on our mistakes rather than forget them and move on which you know you should do!

1. Get some very lively music ready to play loudly. I personally find big band music is best for this!
2. Think of the episode or event that you are dwelling on; think of it lightly and not in detail.
3. Now switch on that big band music and as you lightly run through the event in your mind listen to the music.
4. Repeat this process until the emotions have been washed away and you have established a link between the uplifting music and the memory.

This is a useful tool when you find yourself mulling something over and over 'when you know you shouldn't'. It stops you pushing your mood down and punishing yourself when all you need to say is 'sorry' or just accept that you're human and we all get it wrong sometimes. Once you have removed the negative sting from the memory, often the mind gets bored and leaves the memory alone!

Exercise - Dragon Breathing

I love this exercise and many of my clients and students have found it really useful as a quick stress buster. It's great for clearing out anything from irritation through to anger before it is allowed to grow and root!

1. Face a window or if possible go outside. If you are not able to go outside fill a sink with water and breathe your fire breath into the water!

Then pull the plug when you have finished and watch the water drain way.

2. Take a deep breath in, feel your tummy push out and imagine you are gathering up all of your irritation (or whatever emotion you want to get rid of). Breathe out hard and imagine your breath coming out like a gush of fire releasing all of that angst back into the air (or into the water) to balance the feelings.

3. Do this 3 times.

4. Relax and carry on. You'll notice your feelings have cleared. I choose to do this with anger but you can do it with any other negative emotions that are getting in your way too.

Learning is an art form; just like an artist you need to be able select the right colour and shade. Why choose a dark, heavy colour when a bright colour is always available?

ChapWellian saying circa 846

The previous two exercises are really helpful little tools to clear those emotions that come up every now and then because we are just human. However, if you feel emotions keep coming up and you are constantly putting a plaster on the same whoosh of negative emotion, the next exercise can help you clear away the root cause.

Exercise - Breaking Emotional Triggers

Every few days check in with your emotions and thoughts.
Reflect on what has happened and any emotions or thoughts you have experienced. This is not about blame, it is about self-awareness and keeping your emotions and thoughts working for you, not against you.

If there any emotions or thoughts that do not support your wellbeing write them down. It's good to write them down as it gets them out and away from you, starting the process of moving away from them!

Write down whatever comes to your mind, emotion or thought, that's fine. Make sure you write them on a separate piece of paper so you can reinforce your releasing of these events and emotions by destroying the notes.

Here's an example taken from my own day!

My thoughts – *Increasing frustration spending time on the phone being passed from one service to another and nothing solved. Just wanting to get on with writing but also needing to sort out some banking.*

My emotions – *This is anger in all its aspects – frustration, irritation.*

To release this anger or toxic build-up I would then do a quick 5 minute exercise clearing my angst through relaxation and self-hypnosis. This makes sure it doesn't build and I don't cause problems elsewhere in my world. I'm fairly sure you know what I mean, where the anger arises up again, probably in a non-related situation and causing lots of other problems. This is exactly what I mean by the last straw syndrome where your reactions to something or someone appear to be totally out of proportion to the actual event or situation.

The next exercise is a quick 2 to 5 minute exercise that clears out any unhelpful emotions and reactions. I very much recommend you do this every few days and not just after a stressful, not so good day! Not only does it clear the mind, it also stops the events of the last few days creating roadblocks in the mind for tomorrow! After you have done the exercise get rid of your notes. Either burn them, shred them or enjoy tearing them into small pieces. However you choose to destroy them is fine, just make sure you do it to help reinforce that you are 'getting rid' of the emotions from the past event.

It is important to be aware that you are not clearing the memory or thoughts, just the negative emotions that YOU have created around a situation or event. This doesn't mean you now think whatever is causing the emotions is OK or not worth dealing with; maybe it is, maybe it isn't. It allows you to learn, reflect, make decisions based on what you need and want rather than decisions and actions based on an emotional reaction probably coming from fear.

Exercise - Quick Clearing Technique

Key Points

- **Power Breaths**

- **Comfy chair**

- **Power hose**

- **Drain out of the body**

As usual make sure you are safe to 'switch off' from the outside world for about 5 minutes.

1. Get yourself comfortable.

2. **Power Breaths** – Using your 3 breaths exercise to relax. Breathe in counting 1, 2, 3, pause and out 3, 2, 1, pause. Repeat for 6 to 9 breaths.

3. Start to feel your body relax and count yourself down your 10 step staircase to your safe place. Feel your body relaxing increasingly as you go down each step.

4. Go through your door into your safe place. Look around and enjoy the deep sense of relaxation that your safe place gives you.

5. When you are ready sit in your comfy chair. Remember you are totally safe. Enjoy that feeling of relaxation, safety and calm as you enjoy your own personal space.

6. Feel the relaxation and peace flow through your body. Feel your body being supported by your chair and for a few moments enjoy that feeling of relaxation.

7. Ask yourself, what are the emotions and feelings that need clearing?

8. Accept what comes up and as it comes into your mind imagine you are holding a power hose of tremendous strength. Direct the power hose at the emotions and feelings that need clearing.

9. Switch your power hose on and watch the emotions and feelings wash away and drain out of your mind and body. Whatever feels right for you.

10. When you have cleansed away all traces of the emotions/feelings you wish to clear, imagine throwing the hose behind you.

11. Notice how comfortable you are sitting in your comfy chair in your safe place. Enjoy the comfort of your chair and continue to relax for as long as you want. When you are ready come back into the now.

Now you have a technique which will help you to release those emotions that can cloud your thinking and decisions and work against your overall wellbeing.

Letting go of people and relationship triggers

Sometimes it is not necessarily the negative emotions we hold onto from a past event or time but the actual people. Have you ever held a grudge, blamed someone, known they did you a disservice and kept your emotions and upset alive over their role in your life? Maybe you still do. Maybe it's not a person but a thing. I know my own antagonism towards cancer charities and fundraising for them was a real physical reaction for me following my husband's death; I was refusing to do anything for their causes as they didn't help my husband. It may sound dreadful but that was how I felt. Just like many others react in the opposite way and decide to dedicate their free time to supporting cancer charities so others can be helped. It's not about logic, it's about emotions and feelings driving us. It's about the mind deciding 2 and 2 make 5. Logically I knew cancer charities are a very good thing but emotionally I had piled my hurt and anger on them and the loss of my husband. Accepting and clearing those emotions and feelings that were getting in my way was an important part of accepting my loss. I am happy to say I have just sponsored two friends to run for a cancer charity and am in full support of their endeavours and am even considering doing something myself!

On another occasion I worked with a man in his forties who made reference to his dreadful childhood and how he had made sure he was over his past. I asked how he knew that and he said he always made sure he did the opposite with his children than was done to him. When I suggested that his childhood experiences were dictating his decisions in the now he became angry and said he was the total opposite to his father. I'm sure you get the point here.

The next exercise allows you to break any negative emotional links with a person from your past or present. Once you have broken that negative emotional link it enables you to see them as they are and decide for yourself if you wish to keep them in your life or release them from your mind and life.

Eleanor Roosevelt said, '*No one can put you down without your full permission.*' Guess what? The same applies to the wide range of emotional responses we have!

Are you allowing people from your past to clutter up your emotional closet? Do you get them out to reinforce whatever feelings you are experiencing, maybe poor me, victim, helpless, blame and all those other negative thought patterns?

- Someone who treated you badly

- Someone you let you down

- Someone who made you feel inferior

- Someone who betrayed your trust

- Someone who took away your confidence

- Someone who made you feel not good enough

The past is gone and can only affect us if we choose to hang on to those feelings and use them to reinforce negative feelings in our minds, creating and attracting more of those negative feelings. It is the law of attraction: what you focus on grows and you get more of it. Have you noticed similar patterns, events or people turning up in your life?

Repeating and replaying past hurts and disappointments in the mind keeps them alive and, worse still, keeps you a victim of your own mind and making! Now why would you choose to do that? Remember the past is useful for learning about life, creating experience and using that learning to build the future you deserve. You tried one way and it didn't work so try another. If you keep doing the same thing you'll just get the same stuff. Now why would anyone want that unless they had the life they wanted? Do you? Or have you learnt by now it's you who can choose to enjoy the jungle or build your own cage?

Exercise - Clear Up Past Drama

Exercise Part 1

Key Points

- **Power breaths**

- **Comfy chair**

- **Cut the cord**

- **Say goodbye**

This is a simple exercise to clear away negative links to people from your past and your present. Things happen and we all know we need to move on and develop healthier relationships with those we choose to keep in our lives, or to really move on and stop keeping them in our lives through our actions and thoughts.

1. Power Breaths – On the in breath slowly count 1, 2, 3, pause and on the out breath slowly count 1, 2, 3, pause. It may help to put your hands on your tummy to feel it rise and make sure you take a deep breath.

2. Allow your breathing to gradually return to normal.

3. Now imagine walking down your 10 step staircase, counting each step as you go down to the bottom. The staircase can be exactly as you want it, it's your staircase so enjoy going down the 10 steps!

4. At the bottom of the stairs is a door, open the door and go into the room or place you see, feel or sense. Notice your lovely comfy chair and sink into it.

5. Enjoy the feeling of peace and calm in your special place.

6. See the person standing in front of you; see the cord that joins you stretching from you to them.

7. Reach into your pocket and get out a really heavy, strong, sharp pair of scissors or anything that comes to your mind that you would use to cut something tough, easily and cleanly.

8. Now cut through the cord, all the way through. Watch the cord that joins you shrivel back to you and notice it shrivels back to them and heals as if it never existed between you.

9. Now smile and wave as you watch them wave and smile as they turn and leave your special place.

10. When you are ready bring yourself back to the now, look around, remember what you were doing before, stretch and bring that feeling of relaxation and peace back with you.

You will have gone deeper into trance with this exercise so make sure you give yourself plenty of time to come back into the now. Do not attempt anything until you feel fully awake. It's just like waking up after a light snooze.

Exercise Part 2

Whenever you think about the situation, and as you go about your day, you can do some powerful work to reinforce your new thought pattern. This does not have to take long.

Over the next few days take a few minutes, every now and then, get yourself comfortable and, when it is safe for you to do so, close your eyes or just stare at a fixed point.

Key Points

• **Power Breaths**

• **Imagine the person**

• **Cut the cord**

1. Power Breaths – On the in breath slowly count 1, 2, 3, pause and on the out breath slowly count 1, 2, 3, pause. It may help to put your hands on your tummy to feel it rise and make sure you take a deep breath.

2. Imagine you are standing in front of the person; see the cord that joins you stretching from you to them.

3. Imagine reaching into your pocket and getting out a really heavy, strong, sharp pair of scissors or anything that comes to your mind that you would use to cut something tough.

4. Imagine cutting through the cord, all the way through. Watch the cord that joins you shrivel back to you and notice it shrivels back to them and heals as if it never existed between you.

5. Now imagine smiling and waving as you turn and leave and notice they return your wave and smile, before they turn and leave.

The same rule applies to this mini exercise: always remember to give yourself time to come back into the now before carrying on with what you were doing. By now maybe you are tired of me saying that, but each mini exercise requires you to go within, into a light trance-like state, so it is important that you do it when you can safely remove your concentration from your surroundings and allow yourself enough time to come back into the now fully alert.

Keep your rucksack light for your jungle journey

Within this book I have introduced you to the ChapWell Method and the 7 keys to success, happiness and wellbeing. We have only just begun on the multitude of exercises and techniques that you can easily learn and use to enable you to stop lugging around the past, and create more of what you want for your life journey.

Peace and calm

The first key for me is important and I want to remind you to start with that one to allow your mind to give you a break, allow you to think through what you want to create and what you want to leave in your past. However, if you want to start with any of the other keys then that is fine; it's your life and your choice and you will know best what you need. So enjoy and good luck.

Remember: no trying, just doing

This is a mantra for me and anyone who has worked with me will recognise me saying, forget the trying; all you'll create is more trying. Watch your language from now on as you are doing the exercises; you are making things happen for you exactly as you want. Be aware your mind is also listening to everything you say, so anything negative you say contributes to a negative mindset whereas anything positive creates a 'can-do' mindset. What do you want, positive thoughts or negative? No perfects either; that just comes from our trying approach too!

Be inclusive, not exclusive

Many of my clients have already studied and used other approaches to supporting their wellbeing, creating the life they choose. My message is always the same: if those tools work for you, keep using them and add them to the tools you have now from the 7 keys. The ChapWell Method is all about combining techniques and will add beautifully to those tricks and techniques you have already learnt to keep you travelling along your jungle journey and out of your cage! At a recent speaking engagement I had a heckler who asked, does that include my daily bottle of wine too? The answer is obvious: I am talking about what builds us up long term and doesn't give us any nasty paybacks further down the line. Although my belief is that a little of what we fancy does, in fact, do us good. I'm sure you have your own philosophy; just make sure it is yours and not someone else's. That is just giving our power away: the power to choose success, happiness and wellbeing, or just settle for what we have been led to believe from those influences that we have chosen to listen to.

And there's more for you

I love to hear from people who are following the ChapWell Method, how they are getting along, and encourage you to keep in touch. Let me know how things are going for you via my website www.chapwellmethod.com. Sign up for my free, monthly newsletter where I feature exercises in response to followers' requests, enabling you to add to the wealth of techniques and tools you already have for free. Send in your requests for specific exercises to support your progress. I pick one a month and design an exercise to help keep you growing on the road to your success, happiness and wellbeing.

And more ...

Take your journey further and join a course or contact me to talk about one-to-one, private sessions. Visit the ChapWell method website for more information on the range of courses and sign up to join fellow jungle travellers.

Good luck and enjoy

Finally all that remains for me to say in this book is thank you for taking the time to delve deeper into the ChapWell Method. Enjoy your journey through life, the good and not so good times. Keep in touch and let me know how things go for you.

I leave you with some fine words from Helen Keller, which for me are something of a mantra; I believe either a big or small adventure is what we all need every now and then!

'Life is either a daring
adventure or nothing.'

My Recommended Reading List

I love books, for me they are a source of entertainment, amusement, knowledge, understanding, connection and the list goes on and on. So I wanted to share my favourite books with you which one way or another have come to mean a lot to me. These books sit on the special, top shelf of my office bookcase as dear friends. Not one of these books hold all of the answers for me yet together they have definitely shaped my thinking and continue to support me in the best possible way. If I am stuck in my thinking, wanting a short brain refresh or looking for a new way forward for me or a client I know I'll find the answer from the books on my 'special top shelve'.

Note there is no particular order to my list below it's just how they are placed on my special bookshelf!

Women Who Run with the Wolves by Clarissa Pinkola Estes, PH.D

The 7 Habits of Highly Effective People by Stephen R. Covey

Feel the Fear and Do it Anyway by Susan Jeffers

Effective Leadership by James Adair

Winnie-the-Pooh - The Complete Collection of Stories and Poems by A. A. Milne

Working with Emotional Intelligence by Daniel Goleman

Who Moved My Cheese: An Amazing Way to Deal with Change in Your Work and in Your Life by Dr Spencer Johnson

The One Minute Manager by Kenneth Blanchard & Spencer Johnson

The Art of Happiness by HH Dalai Lama & Howard C Cutler

The Alchemist by Paulo Coelho

The Power is Within You by Louise L. Hay

A New Earth: Create a Better Life by Eckhart Tolle

Gone with the Wind by Margaret Mitchell